THE RAW KITCHEN

★ ★

Energising, Surprising & Yummy

150
GREAT RECIPES

★

CONTENTS

INTRODUCTION

Raw food ... what the? If you thought cooking was key to the whole 'what's for dinner?' caper, you're about to have your eyes opened to a new way of eating. Raw food is the latest food trend and there's good reason why. Surprising perhaps, but it's thought that cooked foods are harder to digest than raw foods. Some experts say that cooking reduces the value of the nutrients in our food. Raw food is also thought to be more alkaline, with less chance of fermenting in the gut. And gut health is important. It's thought to be the breeding ground of inflammation and associated autoimmune reactions.

So what exactly is a raw food diet? It depends who you ask. Generally though, raw foodies tend to consume a diet based on raw fruit, vegetables, nuts, seeds and sprouted grains. Often raw foodists are vegan – but it isn't one and the same. A uniting principle is to avoid consumption of processed foods. Anything that's been pasteurised, homogenised, or produced with the use of synthetic pesticides, chemical fertilisers, industrial solvents or chemical food is out of bounds.

You would be forgiven for assuming that raw foodists don't cook their food and that's more or less true, although food may be warmed to temperatures less than 45°C (115°F). The idea is that below this temperature food retains its vital enzymes, vitamins and minerals.

You'll find raw food principles generally adhered to in this book, but we do make some exceptions.

This is not a vegan cookbook and you will find a small number of recipes that include raw meat and fish.

Occasionally we've included ingredients not strictly raw – rice paper (to make rice paper rolls) for instance, has been steamed, but we've gone with the principle that it's a healthy, non-processed food that's almost raw.

Likewise, maple syrup is not raw. It's heated for long periods, but it's low in fructose and otherwise an excellent and delicious sweetener. If you want to stick to a raw sweetener, use agave syrup instead. It can be substituted every time you see maple syrup in this book.

Vanilla extract is not raw either. Substitute with the real thing – vanilla beans – for a 100% raw version. Similarly soy sauce or the gluten-free version, tamari, is not raw. If you want the raw version, choose nama shoyu soy sauce or coconut amino acids. Huh? That's what Google is for!

Sometimes ingredients do need to be melted or heated in order to facilitate the chemical reaction required in the recipe. To that end, we've occasionally melted chocolate, boiled water to use for pickling and melted agar to create a perfect non-dairy mozzarella cheese. Avoid this handful of recipes if you are 100% raw.

Raw foodies are known for experimentation as they try to emulate the cooked foods that they are used to eating. Cheese is a great example and there are some amazing vegan cheese recipes in this book. Likewise, you don't need to deprive yourself of yoghurt or cream. Try the coconut yoghurt or cashew cream instead – they're delicious!

You'll find both cacao powder and cocoa powder in this book. You might be wondering what the difference is. Raw cacao powder is made by cold-pressing unroasted cocoa beans and removing the fat (to make cacao butter). Cocoa powder is raw cacao that's been roasted at high temperatures.

If you are looking to adopt a raw food diet, or simply want to make the most of the recipes in this book, there are two pieces of kit to consider investing in. A spiraliser will make knocking up those zoodles (zucchini noodles) that bit easier, and a dehydrator will make light work of preparing cookies, crackers and pizza bases. But it's not essential. The most important equipment in raw cooking is the determination to give it a go. So go!

BASICS

RAW GOAT'S CHEESE

INGREDIENTS

15 cups (3.75L, 1 gallon) raw goat's milk

Pinch of mesophilic cheese culture

3 drops rennet, dissolved in ¼ cup (60ml, 2fl oz) water

Pinch of sea salt

METHOD

1. Place the goat's milk in a large saucepan over a low heat and, using a thermometer, heat to 22°C (72°F). Remove from heat.

2. Add the cheese culture and stir gently, then add the rennet solution and salt and stir once again to combine.

3. Cover and set aside at room temperature for 12 hours.

4. Layer a large glass or ceramic bowl with cheesecloth.

5. Gently scrape the curds and whey into the bowl. Fold the cheesecloth up and tie the ends together or secure with rubber bands.

6. Suspend the cheesecloth over the bowl using a wooden spoon or other hanging device. Allow to drain for 6-24 hours to achieve desired consistency.

KOMBUCHA

INGREDIENTS

8 cups (2L, 4pt) water

16 tea bags

2 cups (440g, 1lb) sugar

1 scoby (symbiotic culture of bacteria and yeast, available at healthfood stores)

METHOD

1. Place water, tea bags and sugar in a large saucepan over medium-high heat and bring to the boil. Remove from the heat and allow to steep. Set aside until the tea has cooled to room temperature. Hot tea will destroy the scoby.

2. When tea has completely cooled strain it over glass jar or kombucha urn, discarding the tea bags.

3. With clean hands, gently place the scoby at the top of the jar or urn.

4. Cover the jar or urn with a muslin cloth and secure with an elastic band.

5. Put the jar in a warm corner of the kitchen and leave to ferment for 7 days.

6. Pour kombucha into sealable jars and store in the fridge until ready to drink.

7. Transfer the scoby to a fresh batch of tea and start again!

ALMOND MILK

INGREDIENTS

1 cup (125g, 4oz)
raw almonds

Water, for soaking

2 cups (500ml, 1pt) water

Pinch of sea salt

Honey or maple syrup,
to taste (optional)

METHOD

1. Place the nuts in bowl or glass jar and cover with about 2cm (1in) water. Cover with a plate or a clean tea towel and allow to soak at room temperature for 12-24 hours. Soaking for longer will result in creamier milk.

2. Drain nuts and rinse well under cool water. Discard the soaking liquid.

3. Place the almonds, water and salt in a blender and process for 1 minute, until smooth and creamy.

4. Strain the almonds. Line the strainer with an opened nut bag or cheesecloth, and place over a measuring cup or bowl. Pour the almond mixture into the strainer and press with the back of a spoon to extract all the milk. If using a nut bag, squeeze to extract as much almond milk as possible.

5. Add honey or maple syrup to taste, if using.

   Note: Refrigerate almond milk. Store in sealed containers in the fridge for 2-3 days.

COCONUT YOGHURT

INGREDIENTS

3 young coconuts, or 450g (1lb) raw coconut meat plus 1 cup (250ml, 8fl oz) coconut water

Probiotic powder (equivalent to 2 capsules)

METHOD

1. Sterilise a blender, spatula, spoon and glass bowl by boiling or washing them in very hot water.

2. Crack open coconuts and pour out the water into a jug. Set aside.

3. Scoop out the coconut meat using a spoon. Pick off any remaining husk from the meat and then place it in the blender.

4. Set the blender on medium speed and gradually add the reserved coconut water until the desired consistency is reached.

5. Use a spatula to scrape the mixture into the glass bowl. Sprinkle the probiotic powder onto the yoghurt. Stir with a rubber spatula until combined.

6. Cover the bowl with a cheesecloth and secure with a rubber band. Set aside in a cool, dark place to ferment for 24 hours.

7. Taste, and if still too sweet, allow fermentation to continue until desired tanginess is reached.

   Note: Will keep for 4-5 days in refrigerator. Add honey, vanilla or other flavouring as desired.

KALE CHIPS

INGREDIENTS

1 bunch kale

1 lemon, juiced

1 tbsp agave syrup

2 tbsps nutritional yeast

¼ tsp turmeric powder

½ tsp sea salt

METHOD

1. Rinse the kale and spin dry or dry with a clean tea towel. Remove the tough stems and tear into bite-size pieces.

2. Place the remaining ingredients in a large bowl and mix to combine.

3. Add the kale to the bowl and using clean hands rub the seasoning well into the leaves.

4. Place kale on dehydrator trays and set dehydrator to 45°C (115°F).

5. Dehydrate for 12 hours or until completely dry. Turn then dehydrate again for a further 5 hours or until crispy.

CASHEW CREAM

INGREDIENTS

1 cup (125g, 4oz)
raw cashews

½ cup (125ml, 4fl oz)
water, plus more for
soaking

Savoury cream

½ tsp sea salt

½ lemon, juiced

Sweet cream

1 tbsp maple syrup

½ tsp vanilla extract

Pinch of sea salt

METHOD

1. Place cashews in a bowl and completely cover with water. Set aside to soak for at least one hour. Drain and rinse.

2. Place cashews in a high-speed blender. For savoury cream, add sea salt and lemon, or, for sweet cream, add maple syrup, vanilla extract and salt. Process until smooth and creamy.

Note: Store in the refrigerator for 3-4 days.

SPROUTED HUMMUS

INGREDIENTS

2 cups (400g, 14oz) chickpeas

4 tbsps raw tahini

½ lemon, juiced

2-3 tbsps olive oil

4 cloves garlic, minced

3 tbsps ground cumin

1 tsp sea salt

½ cup (125ml, 4fl oz) water

Olive oil, to garnish

METHOD

1. To sprout the chickpeas, begin by placing them in a large bowl and covering with water. Set aside, covered, for 24 hours. Then rinse and drain chickpeas twice daily for a further 3-4 days until small sprouts are visible.

2. Place sprouted chickpeas, tahini, lemon juice, olive oil, garlic, cumin and salt in the bowl of a food processor and pulse until roughly combined.

3. Gradually add water to the mixture and process until smooth and of the desired consistency (you may not need all the water).

4. Season to taste with extra salt, cumin and lemon juice.

5. Garnish with olive oil and serve.

EDAMAME DIP

INGREDIENTS

3 tbsps extra virgin olive oil

2 cups (315g, 11oz) shelled raw edamame beans

2 cups (60g, 2oz) baby spinach leaves

1 lemon, juiced

3 tbsps tahini

¼ small onion, roughly chopped

2 cloves garlic

¼ tsp ground cumin

1 tsp sea salt

1 cup (15g, ½ oz) fresh basil (retain a few leaves to garnish)

METHOD

1. Place the oil, edamame, spinach, lemon juice, tahini, onion, garlic, cumin, salt and basil into a high-speed blender or food processor. Process on a high speed for 1-2 minutes, until the desired consistency is reached, stopping occasionally to scrape down the sides.

2. Taste and adjust with seasonings as required. Garnish with fresh basil.

MACADAMIA NUT CHEESE

INGREDIENTS

2 cups (250g, 8oz) raw macadamias

½ tsp salt

2 tsps nutritional yeast

1 tsp probiotic powder

1 tsp lemon juice

METHOD

1. Place the macadamia nuts in a bowl and cover with water. Cover and set aside to soak for 6 hours or overnight. Drain and rinse.

2. Place nuts in a high-speed blender and process until very smooth.

3. Line a colander with cheesecloth and place on top of a plate.

4. Scrape the mixture into the colander and fold the cloth over the top. Place a weight on top (jars filled with water will do), just heavy enough to apply pressure but not to push the mixture through the cloth.

5. Set aside at room temperature for 24-48 hours.

6. Add the salt, nutritional yeast, probiotic powder and lemon juice to the macadamias and stir to combine.

7. Scrape the mixture into a cheese mould or plastic container. Transfer to the freezer for 3-4 hours.

Notes: to create a rind, the cheese can be placed in a dehydrator at 43°C (110°F) for 24 hours after freezing.

Cashew nuts may be used in place of macadamia nuts in this recipe.

Store in an airtight container in the fridge for 5-7 days.

ESSENE BREAD

INGREDIENTS

⅓ cup (40g, 1½ oz) walnuts

⅓ cup (40g, 1½ oz) sunflower seeds

1 cup (180g, 6oz) sprouted rye berries

1 cup (180g, 6oz) sprouted wheat berries

½ cup (75g, 3oz) ground linseed

1 tbsp fennel seeds

½ tbsp caraway seeds

½ tbsp cumin seeds

1 tsp dried oregano

1 tsp sea salt

3 tbsps extra virgin olive oil

METHOD

1. Place the walnuts and sunflower seeds in a bowl and cover with water. Cover and set aside in a cool dark place to soak overnight. Drain and rinse.

2. Place the walnuts, sunflower seeds, rye berries, wheat berries and linseed in a food processor and process until coarsely ground.

3. Transfer to a large bowl and add the fennel, caraway and cumin seeds, dried oregano, salt and olive oil. Stir to combine. Cover the bowl with a clean kitchen towel and set aside to rest for 30 minutes.

4. Using hands, form the dough into a loaf shape and transfer to dehydrator tray or baking tray. If using an oven, preheat to the lowest setting.

5. Place in the oven or dehydrator set at (45°C) 115°F for 2 hours. If using an oven, keep the door slightly ajar.

LINSEED CHIPS

INGREDIENTS

2 cups (300g, 10oz) whole linseed

2 cups (500ml, 1pt) water (for soaking)

¼ cup (60ml, 2fl oz) tamari (or liquid aminos)

¼ tsp cayenne pepper (optional)

⅓ cup (15g, ½ oz) fresh coriander

⅔ cup (40g, 1½ oz) sun-dried tomatoes

1 tbsp olive oil

1 tsp sea salt

METHOD

1. Place the linseed into a bowl and cover with the water. Set aside to soak for 30 minutes. Drain and rinse, then place the swollen seeds back in the bowl. Stir in the tamari.

2. Place the cayenne pepper, coriander, tomatoes, oil and salt in a food processor and process until pureed.

3. Add pureed mixture to the linseed and stir well to combine..

4. Spread mixture in an even layer onto dehydrator sheets and dehydrate at 45°C (115°F) for 4 hours until dry.

5. Break into pieces and return to the dehydrator for a further 5 hours until crispy.

BUFFALO MOZZARELLA

INGREDIENTS

1 cup (125g, 4oz) raw cashews

1 cup (250ml, 8fl oz) plain coconut yoghurt (see recipe page 12)

½ cup (125ml, 4fl oz) water

1 tsp sea salt

3½ tbsps tapioca flour (or cornflour)

1 tbsp agar powder, dissolved in ½ cup (125ml, 4fl oz) boiling water

METHOD

1. Place the cashew nuts in a bowl and cover with water. Set aside to soak for 4-6 hours. Drain and rinse.

2. Place the yoghurt, cashew nuts, water and salt in a high-speed blender and process until very smooth, creamy and completely blended.

3. Remove mixture from blender into a plastic or glass container. Cover loosely and set aside at room temperature for a minimum of 12 hours (and up to 24). The mixture should be tart to taste.

4. Add the tapioca flour and stir to combine.

5. Pour the dissolved agar powder into a large saucepan over medium-high heat. Cover and bring to a boil. Remove the lid and allow to simmer gently for 3 minutes, then add the yoghurt mixture and whisk. Continue to cook, stirring constantly, until the mixture is smooth and shiny. The mixture should not be grainy. If it is, continue cooking until it is smooth.

6. Make ready a large bowl of iced water. Using a spoon or ice-cream scoop, drop balls of the mixture into the bowl. Allow to sit for 30 minutes, or until firm.

Note: store in the refrigerator in brine (salted water) or olive oil.

TWO TOMATO PESTO

INGREDIENTS

½ cup (25g, 1oz) sun-dried tomatoes

1-2 fresh tomatoes, roughly chopped

2 tbsps pumpkin seeds

2 tbsps almond crumble (see recipe page 33)

3 tbsps virgin olive oil

1 clove garlic

1 tsp mixed dried herbs

¼ tsp sea salt

½ tsp fresh black pepper

¼ cup (10g, ¼ oz) fresh basil leaves, rough chopped

METHOD

1. Place the sun-dried tomatoes in a small bowl and cover with warm water. Set aside.

2. Place the fresh tomatoes, pumpkin seeds, almond crumble, olive oil, garlic, mixed herbs and salt and black pepper in a high-speed blender or food processor. Pulse until a coarse paste forms.

3. Drain the sun-dried tomatoes, retaining the water.

4. Add sun-dried tomatoes to the blender or food processor and process to form a paste. Gradually add the retained water to achieve desired consistency.

5. Add basil and pulse to combine.

TOFU SOUR CREAM

INGREDIENTS

350g (12oz) silken tofu

¼ cup (60ml, 2fl oz) lemon juice

½ tsp rice vinegar

1 tsp garlic, minced (optional)

¼ tsp sea salt

METHOD

1. Place all ingredients in a food processor or high-speed blender, and process until well combined.

2. Taste and adjust with lemon juice, vinegar or salt as desired.

CASHEW CHILLI NUT CHEESE

INGREDIENTS

2 cups (250g, 8oz) raw cashew nuts

1 cup (250ml, 8fl oz) water

1 tsp probiotic powder

1 tbsp lemon juice

1 tsp raw, unprocessed salt (or special cheese salt)

1 tsp nutritional yeast (optional)

1 tsp mixed dried herbs

1 tsp chilli flakes, to garnish

METHOD

1. Place the cashew nuts in a bowl and cover with water. Cover and set aside to soak overnight. Drain and rinse.

2. Place cashew nuts and water into a high-speed blender and process until smooth and creamy. Add probiotic powder and lemon juice and process again for 5-10 seconds.

3. Prepare a large bowl by lining with 2-3 layers of cheesecloth.

4. Transfer the cashew mixture onto the cheesecloth, then gather the edges of the cheesecloth and tie the loosely together. Suspend the cheesecloth over the bowl using a long spoon handle.

5. Place the dish in a warm place and leave the cheese culture to ferment for at least 24 hours.

6. Add salt, nutritional yeast, if using, and herbs and gently mix together.

7. Transfer to a cheese form or round dish and refrigerate for 24 hours before serving, garnished with chilli.

MINT COCONUT PESTO

INGREDIENTS

Small piece of fresh
ginger, chopped

2 garlic cloves, roughly
chopped

2 bunches of mint,
leaves picked

⅓ cup (40g, 1½ oz)
sunflower seeds

¼ cup (20g, ¾ oz)
flaked coconut

⅓ cup (80ml, 3fl oz)
extra virgin olive oil
(or coconut oil)

Sea salt and freshly
ground pepper, to taste

METHOD

1. Place the ginger, garlic, mint, sunflower seeds and coconut in a
    blender or food processor. Pulse until a coarse powder forms.

2. Set the motor to slow and gradually add the olive or coconut oil
    in a thin stream. Add salt and pepper and blend for a further few
    seconds until combined.

SERVES 1½ CUPS ★ PREP 15MIN

BASIL PESTO

INGREDIENTS

1 bunch basil, leaves picked

½ cup (60g, 2oz) pine nuts

1 clove garlic, roughly chopped

½ cup (125ml, 4fl oz) extra virgin olive oil

1 tbsp lemon juice

3 tbsps nutritional yeast

Sea salt and freshly ground pepper, to taste

METHOD

1. Place the basil, pine nuts and garlic in a blender or food processor. Pulse until a coarse powder forms.

2. Set the motor to slow and gradually add the olive oil in a thin stream. Add lemon juice, yeast and salt and pepper and blend for a further few seconds until combined.

LINSEED CRACKERS

INGREDIENTS

½ cup (65g, 2oz) pumpkin seeds

½ cup (60g, 2oz) sunflower seeds

½ cup (25g, 1oz) sun-dried tomatoes

2 carrots, roughly chopped

1 garlic clove

½ tsp sea salt

1 tbsp fresh oregano

1 cup (150g, 5oz) ground linseed

¼ cup (40g, 1½ oz) whole linseed

METHOD

1. Place the pumpkin seeds and sunflower seeds in a container and cover with water. Set aside to soak overnight.

2. Soak the sun-dried tomatoes in warm water and set aside for 30 minutes.

3. Place the sun-dried tomatoes, carrots, garlic, salt and oregano in the bowl of a food processor and pulse until smooth.

4. Transfer mixture to a large mixing bowl. Add ground linseed and whole linseed and stir to combine.

5. Drain the soaked seeds and place in the food processor. Gently pulse until seed mixture is coarsely chopped.

6. Pour seeds into the mixing bowl and fold ingredients together until batter is smooth and uniform.

7. Line two or three trays with dehydrator sheets or greaseproof paper. Spoon on batter to a thickness of 5mm (¼ in) and smooth the surface with a spatula.

8. Dehydrate at 40°C (105°F) for 8-10 hours.

9. Gently peel back paper and flip over crackers. Using a sharp knife, score crackers into desired size.

10. Dehydrate for a further 8-10 hours until desired crispness is achieved.

11. When ready, break crackers by snapping along scored lines.

ALMOND BUTTER

INGREDIENTS

2 cups (250g, 8oz) raw almonds (unsalted and unsoaked)

½ tsp sea salt

2 tbsps honey (optional)

METHOD

1. Place the almonds into the bowl of a food processer.

2. Process for 5 minutes, stopping occasionally to scrape the bowl down, until a powder forms.

3. Continue processing almonds for a further 15 minutes. During this time, the butter will first form a dough-like consistency, then appear whipped before forming a buttery consistency.

4. Add salt and honey, if using, and stir until combined.

5. Transfer butter to a jar and store in the fridge.

SERVES 1½ CUPS ★ PREP 10MIN

ALMOND CRUMBLE

INGREDIENTS

1 cup (125g, 4oz) raw almonds

1 tbsp nutritional yeast

1 garlic clove, finely chopped

1 tbsp hemp seeds (optional)

¼ tsp sea salt

METHOD

1. Place all the ingredients in a food processor or high-speed blender.

2. Process until a light and fluffy crumble forms.

   Note: store in a sealed container in the fridge.

SEED SNAP CRACKERS

INGREDIENTS

2 cups (300g, 10oz) linseed

2 cups (500ml, 1pt) water, for soaking

⅔ cup (80g, 3oz) sunflower seeds

½ cup (80g, 3oz) sesame seeds

1 tsp sea salt

METHOD

1. Place linseed in a bowl and cover with water. Cover and set aside to soak overnight.

2. Preheat the oven to 40°C (100°F) and line a baking tray with greaseproof paper.

3. Drain linseed and place in a large mixing bowl. Add sunflower seeds, sesame seeds and salt and mix to just combine.

4. Using a wet spatula spread the mixture in an even layer onto the baking paper.

5. Score the mixture with a sharp knife into the desired shape and size of crackers.

6. Transfer to the oven and bake for 1 hour. If the top is dry, turn over and return to the oven for a further 1 hour. If not yet dry, return to the oven and check regularly until dry.

7. Remove from the oven and set aside to cool. Snap into small crackers down the score lines when cool.

SUN-DRIED TOMATO DIP

INGREDIENTS

1 zucchini, peeled and chopped

1 red capsicum, deseeded and roughly chopped

¼ cup (15g, ½ oz) sun-dried tomatoes

1 small clove garlic, roughly chopped

½ cup (115g, 4oz) raw tahini

¼ cup (60ml, 2fl oz) fresh lemon juice

1 tbsp extra virgin olive oil

½ tsp sea salt

¼ tsp red pepper flakes

¼ bunch flat-leaf parsley (retaining some for garnish)

METHOD

1. Place all the ingredients in a high-speed blender or food processor and process until smooth but retaining some coarser texture.

2. Garnish with extra parsley to serve.

CRUNCHY GREEN BEANS

INGREDIENTS

(450g, 1lb) frozen green beans

1 tbsp coconut oil, melted

1 tsp sea salt

2 tsps nutritional yeast

METHOD

1. Remove beans from the freezer and place in a bowl. Set aside to thaw slightly.

2. Pour coconut oil over the beans and add salt and yeast. Stir to fully coat.

3. Transfer to the dehydrator or oven set at the lowest temperature for 12-14 hours until crispy.

KALE PESTO

INGREDIENTS

1 cup (125g, 4oz) raw pistachios, soaked overnight

1 bunch kale, leaves picked

1 garlic clove, chopped

½ cup (125ml, 4fl oz) virgin olive oil

½ lime, juiced

Sea salt and freshly ground black pepper, to taste

METHOD

1. Place the pistachios in a bowl and cover with water. Set aside to soak overnight. Drain and rinse.

2. Place the kale and garlic in a blender or food processor. Pulse until a coarse powder forms.

3. Set the motor to slow and gradually add the olive oil in a thin stream. Add lime juice and salt and pepper and blend for a further few seconds until combined.

PISTACHIO LEMON BUTTER

INGREDIENTS

2 cups (250g, 8oz) raw
pistachios, shelled

1 lemon, juiced

½ tsp sea salt

METHOD

1. Place the pistachios into the bowl of a food processer.

2. Process for 5 minutes, stopping occasionally to scrape the bowl
    down, until a powder forms.

3. Add lemon juice and continue processing nuts for a further 15
    minutes. During this time, the butter will first form a dough-
    like consistency, then appear whipped before forming a buttery
    consistency.

4. Add salt and stir until combined.

5. Transfer butter to a jar and store in the fridge.

AVOCADO HUMMUS

INGREDIENTS

1 zucchini, roughly chopped

1 avocado, quartered

1 lemon, freshly squeezed

2-3 cloves garlic

¼ tsp sea salt

2 tsps ground cumin

½ cup (115g, 4oz) tahini

METHOD

1. Place the zucchini and avocado in a food processor or blender and pulse to roughly combine.

2. Add the lemon juice, garlic, salt, cumin and tahini and process to the desired consistency. Stop to scrape mixture down the side of the bowl occasionally.

3. Season to taste with additional garlic, cumin and salt.

BREAKFAST

OVERNIGHT RASPBERRY CHIA POTS

INGREDIENTS

1 cup (125g, 4oz)
fresh raspberries

1 orange, peeled and
pith removed , roughly
chopped

1½ cups (375ml, 13fl oz)
almond milk

¼ cup (40g, 1½ oz)
white chia seeds

1 tsp vanilla extract

2 kiwi fruit, peeled
and diced

2 tbsps maple syrup

Fresh mint

METHOD

1. Using a high-speed blender, process the raspberries (reserving a few to serve), orange and half of the almond milk until smooth.

2. Divide the mixture between two serving jars or glasses, then pour half the remaining almond milk, chia seeds and vanilla extract into each jar.

3. Cover and transfer to the refrigerator for 1 hour. Stir and then return to the refrigerator overnight.

4. To serve, pile kiwi fruit and fresh raspberries on top of each pot, drizzle over maple syrup and garnish with fresh mint.

CITRUS WATER WITH MINT

INGREDIENTS

4 cups (1L, 2pt)
filtered water

1 orange, sliced

1 lemon, sliced

1 lime, sliced

1 sprig mint

Ice

METHOD

1. Finely slice the orange, lemon and lime and place in a jug.

2. Pour over the water and transfer to the refrigerator to chill overnight.

3. Serve in glasses with ice and garnished with mint.

CEREAL BARS

INGREDIENTS

⅔ cup (150g, 5oz)
almond butter
(see recipe page 32)

½ cup (180g, 6oz)
malt rice syrup

¼ tsp sea salt

1½ cups (130g, 4½ oz)
rolled oats

1 cup (25g, 1oz)
rice puffs

3 tbsps cornflakes,
crushed

1 cup (25g, 1oz)
quinoa puffs

METHOD

1. Line a shallow baking dish with foil or plastic wrap.

2. Combine the nut butter, syrup and sea salt in a large bowl.

3. Add the oats and cereals and mix together until ingredients are well combined and sticky. If more moisture is required, add more syrup.

4. Press the mixture into the baking dish and then cover with another layer of foil or plastic wrap.

5. Transfer to the refrigerator for 4 hours.

6. Remove and cut into bars. Wrap each bar and return to the refrigerator until ready to eat.

CHOCOLATE BUCKWHEAT PORRIDGE

INGREDIENTS

1 cup (170g, 6oz) raw buckwheat groats, soaked

2 tbsps linseed (optional)

1 banana, sliced

½ cup (125ml, 4fl oz) almond milk

2 tbsps raw cacao powder (or unsweetened cocoa powder)

½ tsp vanilla extract

¼ tsp ground cinnamon

1½ tbsps maple syrup

Pinch sea salt

To serve

1 banana, sliced

2 tbsps raw hazelnuts, roughly chopped

1 tbsp desiccated coconut

1 tbsp raw chocolate, grated

METHOD

1. Place buckwheat groats and linseed, if using, into a bowl and cover with water. Set aside to soak for a minimum of 2 hours or overnight if possible. Rinse and drain thoroughly.

2. Place all of the porridge ingredients in a high-speed blender or food processor and process until combined. Process more or less according to your preference for smooth or chunky porridge.

3. Scrape into serving pots or bowls and transfer to the refrigerator to chill for 30 minutes before eating, if desired.

4. To serve, top with slices of banana, chopped hazelnuts, coconut and grated chocolate.

GRAPE SMOOTHIE

INGREDIENTS

1 lemon, juiced

2 cups (400g, 14oz) green seedless grapes, washed

1 medium bunch mint, washed and roughly chopped

½ avocado, peeled and pitted

2 tsps rice malt syrup

1 tbsp chia seeds

1 cup (150g, 5oz) ice cubes

METHOD

1. Add all the ingredients to the blender and process until smooth enough to drink.

2. Pour into glasses. Garnish with mint and a sprinkle of chia seeds and serve immediately.

SERVES 1-2 ★ PREP 10MIN

TURMERIC SPICE SMOOTHIE

INGREDIENTS

1 mango, peeled and pitted

1 cup (200g, 7oz) banana, frozen

¾ cup (185ml, 6fl oz) coconut water

¼ cup (60ml, 2fl oz) coconut yoghurt (see recipe page 12)

1 tsp vanilla extract

2 tsps maple syrup

½ tsp ground tumeric

¼ tsp ground cinnamon

METHOD

1. Add all the ingredients to the blender and process until smooth enough to drink.

2. Pour into glasses and serve immediately.

RAW BUCKWHEAT AND QUINOA PORRIDGE

INGREDIENTS

½ cup (85g, 3oz) raw buckwheat groats

¼ cup (40g, 1½ oz) quinoa

1 banana, sliced

1 tbsp almond butter (see recipe page 32)

1-2 tbsps honey

1 cup (250ml, 8fl oz) unsweetened almond milk

½ tsp ground cinnamon

To serve

1 banana, sliced

¼ cup (30g, 1oz) chopped raw nuts

1 tbsp coconut flakes

METHOD

1. Place buckwheat and quinoa in a large jar or bowl and cover with water. Set aside to soak for a minimum of 2 hours and overnight if possible. Drain and rinse thoroughly.

2. Place all porridge ingredients in a high-speed blender or food processor and process until combined but still chunky.

3. Scrape into serving pots or bowls and transfer to the refrigerator to chill for 30 minutes before eating, if desired.

4. To serve, top with slices of banana, chopped nuts and coconut flakes.

SERVES 2 ★ PREP 10MIN

BERRY SMOOTHIE BOWL

INGREDIENTS

1½ cups (185g, 6oz) raspberries (frozen or fresh)

½ cup (50g, 2oz) blueberries (frozen or fresh)

½ cup (125ml, 4fl oz) coconut yoghurt (see recipe page 12)

1 cup (150g, 5oz) ice cubes

2 tbsps rice malt syrup

1 tbsp lemon juice

To serve

2 tbsps pumpkin seeds

2 tbsps chia seeds

2 tbsps goji berries

2 tbsps sunflower seeds

½ cup (60g, 2oz) fresh berries

METHOD

1. Place ingredients for the smoothie into a blender and process until smooth.

2. Pour the smoothie into 2 bowls and finish with the suggested toppings, or toppings of your choice.

KALE GREEN SMOOTHIE

INGREDIENTS

1 banana (frozen)

1 bunch kale, washed and tough stalks removed

1 cup (250ml, 8fl oz) coconut water

1 tbsp linseed (optional)

Handful fresh mint leaves

1-2 tbsps maple syrup

Pinch of sea salt

½ cup (75g, 3oz) ice cubes

METHOD

1. Add all the ingredients to a blender and process until smooth enough to drink.

2. Pour into glasses and serve immediately.

FRUITY MUESLI BARS

INGREDIENTS

1½ cups (130g, 4½ oz) rolled oats

1 cup (25g, 1oz) quinoa puffs

¼ tsp sea salt

¼ cup (40g, 1½ oz) currants

¼ cup (40g, 1½ oz) sultanas

½ cup (50g, 2oz) rice puffs

½ cup (60g, 2oz) sliced almonds

2 tbsps sesame seeds

¼ cup (60ml, 2fl oz) coconut oil

½ cup (65g, 2oz) almond butter (see recipe page 32)

½ cup (180g, 6oz) malt rice syrup

1 tsp vanilla extract

METHOD

1. Line a shallow baking tray with foil or plastic wrap.

2. Combine the oats, quinoa puffs, salt, currants, sultanas, rice puffs, almonds and sesame seeds in a large bowl.

3. In a medium saucepan over a low heat, melt the coconut oil. Remove from heat and add the almond butter, syrup and vanilla. Stir until smooth then set aside to cool slightly.

4. Pour the wet mixture over the dry mixture and stir to combine well.

5. Press the mixture into the baking tray and then cover with another layer of foil or plastic wrap.

6. Transfer to the freezer for 15 minutes until firm, then remove and cut into bars. Wrap each bar and return to the refrigerator until ready to eat.

FRUIT AND YOGHURT WITH RAW GRANOLA

INGREDIENTS

1 cup (250ml, 8fl oz) coconut yoghurt (see recipe page 12)

10 strawberries, chopped

2 peaches, stoned and chopped

¼ cup (20g, ¾ oz) raw granola (see recipe on page 62)

Mint, to garnish

METHOD

1. Prepare two serving glasses or bowls.

2. Divide half the coconut yoghurt between each glass or bowl.

3. Add a layer of fruit and granola and then another layer of coconut yoghurt.

4. Finish with another layer of fruit and granola and a garnish of fresh mint.

AUTUMN SPICE OVERNIGHT OATS

INGREDIENTS

½ cup (125ml, 4fl oz) unsweetened almond milk

2 tbsps natural salted peanut butter

1 tbsp maple syrup

½ cup (40g, 1½ oz) rolled oats

2 tbsps sultanas or dried cranberries

1 apple, cored and chopped (reserve a few pieces to serve)

To serve

½ tsp cinnamon

1 tbsp sultanas or dried cranberries

METHOD

1. Place the almond milk, peanut butter and maple syrup in a bowl and stir to combine. Add oats, sultanas or cranberries and stir again, ensuring all oats have been coated and covered in milk.

2. Cover securely with plastic wrap and transfer to the refrigerator to soak overnight.

3. Remove from refrigerator and add apple and cinnamon to the bowl. Stir to combine.

4. Transfer to individual serving bowls and top with reserved apple and sultanas or cranberries.

BERRY SMOOTHIE

INGREDIENTS

1 cup (200g, 7oz) blackberries (frozen or fresh)

½ cup (50g, 2oz) blueberries (frozen or fresh)

½ cup (60g, 2oz) raspberries (frozen or fresh)

1 cup (250ml, 8fl oz) coconut water

½ tsp vanilla extract

½ bunch mint leaves, washed

1 cup (150g, 5oz) ice cubes

Mint and additional berries, to garnish

METHOD

1. Add all the ingredients to a blender and blend until smooth enough to drink.

2. Pour into glasses, garnish with fresh herbs and extra berries and serve immediately.

GRANOLA

INGREDIENTS

½ cup (70g, 2½ oz) raw walnuts

½ cup (70g, 2½ oz) raw almonds

½ cup (70g, 2½ oz) raw hazelnuts

½ cup (85g, 3oz) raw buckwheat groats

4 tbsps sunflower seeds

4 tbsps pumpkin seeds

4 tbsps sesame seeds

4 tbsps chia seeds

4 tbsps ground linseed

2 tbsps coconut oil, melted

2 tbsps maple syrup

1 tsp cinnamon

¼ tsp ground cloves

Sea salt, to taste

4 dates, pitted and chopped

2 tbsps sultanas

METHOD

1. Reserve a few handfuls of nuts and seeds and set aside. Place the remaining nuts and seeds (except the ground linseed) in a bowl and cover with water. Set aside to soak for 6 hours. Drain and rinse well. Transfer onto a clean tea towel.

2. Preheat the oven to 45°C (115°F) or prepare the dehydrator. Line a baking tray with greaseproof paper or prepare dehydrator trays.

3. Pat the soaked nuts and seeds dry with a paper towel and then transfer to a high-speed blender or food processor. Process for 10-15 seconds in order to break up the mixture to the desired consistency. Add the linseed, coconut oil, maple syrup, spices and salt and briefly pulse to combine.

4. Mix in the reserved whole nuts and the dried fruit. Spread mixture on prepared trays.

5. Transfer to the oven for 10 hours or a dehydrator for 24 hours or until completely dry and crunchy.

HOMEMADE BLUEBERRY BASIL LEMONADE

INGREDIENTS

6 lemons, peeled

4 cups (1L, 2pts) water

1 cup (350g, 12oz) honey

1 cup (100g, 3½ oz) blueberries (fresh or frozen)

10 basil leaves

To serve

4-5 slices lemon

Handful basil leaves

METHOD

1. Place the lemons, water, honey, blueberries and basil leaves in a high-speed blender. Blend on high for 5 minutes, or until ingredients are completely blended and broken down.

2. Pour the mixture through a mesh strainer set over a large jug. Press with the back of a spoon to squeeze out as much liquid as possible. Discard pulp. Repeat a further one or two times to achieve a clear and pulp-free lemonade.

3. Serve with ice, lemon slices and fresh basil.

SERVES 2 ★ PREP 15MIN

CUCUMBER LEMONADE

INGREDIENTS

1-2 large Continental cucumbers, peeled or unpeeled, cut into large chunks, plus a few slices for garnish

8 lemons, juiced

⅓ cup (70g, 2½ oz) sugar

2 cups (500ml, 1pt) cold sparkling water

To serve

2 stalks basil

Ice

METHOD

1. Place the cucumber in a high-speed blender or food processor and process until completely pureed.

2. Pour the mixture through a mesh strainer set over a large jug. Press with the back of a spoon to squeeze out as much liquid as possible. Discard pulp. Repeat a further one or two times to achieve a clear and pulp-free liquid.

3. Add lemon juice, sugar and water and stir to mix together. Transfer to the refrigerator to chill for 30 minutes. Stir again before serving.

4. Serve with cucumber slices, fresh basil and ice.

CHIA FRESCA

INGREDIENTS

6 cups (1.5L, 50fl oz) cold water

4 lemons, juiced

8-10 drops liquid stevia, or ¼ cup (55g, 2oz) sugar

2 tbsps white and black chia seeds

To serve

6 slices lemon

Handful mint leaves

METHOD

1. Pour the water into a large jug. Add the lemon juice and stevia or sugar. Taste and adjust with more sweetener or lemon juice as desired.

2. Stir the chia seeds into the lemon water and set aside for 10 minutes. Stir occasionally to dislodge any seeds that are stuck on the glass.

3. Pour into glasses and serve with lemon slices and fresh mint.

CREAMY CHIA POTS WITH FROZEN RASPBERRIES

INGREDIENTS

4 tbsps chia seeds

1½ cups (375ml, 13fl oz) coconut milk

½ tsp vanilla extract

Pinch of salt

To serve

½ cup (125ml, 4fl oz) cashew cream (see recipe on page 14)

½ cup (45g, 1½ oz) raw granola (see recipe on page 62)

½ cup (60g, 2oz) raspberries (frozen)

METHOD

1. Place chia seeds, coconut milk, vanilla and salt into a bowl and cover with plastic wrap. Transfer to the refrigerator to soak overnight.

2. When ready to serve, spoon chia seed mixture into serving glasses or bowls and top with a layer of raw granola, cashew cream and frozen raspberries.

SALADS

SERVES 2 ★ PREP 20MIN

MANGO AND GOAT'S CHEESE SALAD

INGREDIENTS

Salad

1 avocado, peeled, seeded and chopped

1 mango, peeled, seeded and chopped

½ cup (60g, 2oz) raw walnuts

Large handful mixed lettuce leaves

100g (3½ oz) goat's cheese (see recipe page 8)

Simple balsamic vinaigrette

¼ cup (60ml, 2fl oz) balsamic vinegar

2 tsps dark brown sugar

1 clove garlic, minced

½ tsp salt

½ tsp freshly ground black pepper

¾ cup (185ml, 6fl oz) olive oil

METHOD

1. Prepare the salad ingredients and arrange on serving plates.

2. Combine the balsamic vinegar, sugar, garlic and salt and pepper in a small mixing bowl. Gradually add the olive oil and whisk until emulsified.

3. Dress the salad and serve immediately.

BEETROOT CARPACCIO WITH WALNUT DRESSING

INGREDIENTS

Salad

1 beetroot

1 golden beetroot

4 tbsps balsamic vinegar

Handful rocket leaves

Walnut oil dressing

¼ cup (60ml, 2fl oz) walnut oil

1 tbsp white wine vinegar

½ tsp sea salt

METHOD

1. Using a mandolin or very sharp knife, peel and slice the beetroots as thinly as possible. Place in a shallow bowl and pour over the balsamic vinegar. Cover and refrigerate overnight.

2. Remove beetroot from the fridge 30 minutes before serving. Drain and bring to room temperature.

3. Arrange beetroot and rocket on the plates and sprinkle with walnuts.

4. Drizzle walnut oil dressing over the salad and serve.

TOMATO SALAD WITH BLACK PEPPER DRESSING

INGREDIENTS

Salad

4 beef tomatoes, cut into wedges

2 spring onions, sliced

½ white onion, diced

Black pepper dressing

3 tbsps extra virgin olive oil

1 tbsp apple cider vinegar

Pinch of salt

1 tsp freshly ground black pepper

1 tsp coriander seeds

METHOD

1. Prepare the salad ingredients and place in a large bowl.

2. Add the dressing ingredients to a small jar with a sealable lid and shake vigorously until well combined, or whisk ingredients together in a small bowl. Season to taste.

3. Add dressing to salad, toss, and serve.

RED CABBAGE COLESLAW

INGREDIENTS

½ head red cabbage

½ cup (20g, ¾ oz) fresh parsley leaves, roughly chopped

1 lemon, juiced

¼ tsp sea salt

¼ tsp black pepper

3 tbsps extra virgin olive oil

METHOD

1. To prepare the cabbage, use a mandolin at the thinnest setting, or grate in a food processor or box grater. Transfer to a large bowl.

2. Add the parsley, lemon juice, salt and pepper to the cabbage and toss to combine.

3. Pour over the olive oil and toss again to fully coat the cabbage.

4. If time allows, sit at room temperature for 20 minutes before serving.

RADISH AND DILL SALAD

INGREDIENTS

Salad

Handful beetroot leaves

A few red romano lettuce leaves

Small handful watercress

1 spring onion, sliced

3-4 radishes, thinly sliced

Few sprigs of dill

Lemon-dill dressing

1 lemon, juiced and zested

1 tbsp fresh dill, finely chopped

½ tsp sea salt

½ tsp Dijon mustard

Freshly ground black pepper

6 tbsps canola oil

METHOD

1. Arrange the salad ingredients on serving plates.

2. Place all dressing ingredients except oil in a medium bowl and whisk to combine. Gradually add the oil, whisking continuously, until completely incorporated. Season to taste.

3. Drizzle dressing over salad and serve immediately.

SERVES 1 ★ PREP 10MIN

CRUNCH LUNCH SALAD

INGREDIENTS

1 pomegranate,
seeds extracted

1 pear, cored and
thinly sliced

2 tbsps raw walnuts

Handful spinach leaves

Macadamia nut cheese
(see recipe page 18)

METHOD

1. To prepare the pomegranate, cut in half and push out the centre a
    bit. Holding over a bowl of water, hit the back of it with a wooden
    spoon to release the seeds into the water.

2. Layer the salad ingredients in a jar.

PEAR AND CASHEW SALAD

INGREDIENTS

Large handful rocket

2 pears, peeled,
cored and chopped

¼ cup (30g, 1oz)
raw cashew nuts

2 tbsps linseed

Balsamic dressing
(see recipe page 92)

METHOD

1. Arrange the rocket leaves, pear and cashew nuts on a serving plate.

2. Sprinkle linseed over the salad.

3. Drizzle with balsamic dressing and serve immediately.

SUMMER FRUITS SALAD

INGREDIENTS

2 large handfuls mixed lettuce leaves

6-8 strawberries

½ cup (50g, 2oz) blueberries

¼ cup (80g, 3oz) dried cranberries

Macadamia nut cheese (see recipe page 18)

1 tbsp grated macadamia nuts, to serve

METHOD

1. Arrange the salad ingredients in serving bowls.

2. Sprinkle with grated macadamia nuts to serve.

ORANGE POPPY SEED DRESSING

INGREDIENTS

2 oranges, freshly squeezed

1 tbsp poppy seeds

1 tsp Dijon mustard

1 tbsp honey

½ tsp salt

¼ tsp pepper

2 tbsps olive oil

METHOD

1. Whisk orange juice, poppy seeds, mustard, honey, salt and pepper together in a small bowl.

2. Pour in the olive oil in a steady stream, whisking constantly, until well combined.

THAI SALAD SPROUTS

INGREDIENTS

Dressing

1 garlic clove

¼ cup (55g, 2oz) raw almond butter (see recipe page 32)

2 tbsps fresh lime juice

2 tbsps nama shoyu soy sauce (or tamari)

2 tbsps water

2 tsps maple syrup

1 tbsp toasted sesame oil

1 tsp ginger, freshly grated

Salad

Handful mini bean sprouts

Handful green sprouts

1 red capsicum, seeded and sliced

1 carrot, julienned

1 large beetroot, julienned

METHOD

1. Place all dressing ingredients in a jar with a sealable lid and shake until thoroughly combined.

2. Place the salad ingredients in a large bowl and pour over dressing. Toss well to coat.

3. Arrange salad on individual plates and serve.

ASIAN SLAW WITH MISO DRESSING

INGREDIENTS

Salad

2 carrots

¼ head small red cabbage

1 spring onion, chopped

1 tbsp black poppy seeds

Miso dressing

¼ cup (60ml, 2fl oz) white (or yellow) miso

3 tbsps agave nectar

¼ cup (55g, 2oz) raw tahini

2 tbsps tamari

2 tsps ginger, grated

½ cup (125ml, 4fl oz) water

METHOD

1. Finely julienne the carrot and red cabbage using a mandolin or very sharp knife.

2. Combine all the slaw ingredients together in a bowl.

3. Combine all the dressing ingredients in a blender or food processor. Process on high until fully combined. Add more water if required to reach the desired consistency.

4. Pour dressing over the slaw and toss well to coat.

WATERMELON RADISH AND ORANGE SALAD

INGREDIENTS

2 watermelon radishes, very thinly sliced

1 orange, peeled, pith removed and chopped

¼ cup (30g, 1oz) raw walnuts

2 tbsps chives, chopped

100g (3½ oz) cashew cheese (see recipe on page 26)

METHOD

1. Arrange the radish and orange on serving plates.

2. Sprinkle with walnuts, chives and cashew cheese.

ROCKET AND RADISH SALAD WITH LINSEED DRESSING

INGREDIENTS

Dressing

3 tbsps linseed

2 tbsps balsamic vinegar

1 tbsp water

1 garlic clove, crushed

¼ tsp brown sugar

¼ tsp sea salt

Salad

Handful rocket

3 baby radishes, sliced

1 Lebanese cucumber, sliced

1 spring onion, sliced

Linseed, to garnish

METHOD

1. Place all dressing ingredients in a jar with a sealable lid and shake until thoroughly combined.

2. Arrange the salad ingredients in serving bowls.

3. Drizzle dressing over the salad and garnish with linseed.

4. Serve immediately.

ORANGE SALAD WITH WALNUTS

INGREDIENTS

2 oranges

¼ cup (30g, 1oz) raw walnuts

Handful mint leaves

METHOD

1. Using a sharp knife, remove the top and the bottom of the orange and cut away the remaining peel and white pith. Slice thickly.

2. Arrange the orange slices on a plate and scatter with walnuts and fresh mint.

LEMON AND HONEY DRESSING

INGREDIENTS

½ cup (125ml, 4fl oz) extra virgin olive oil

4 tbsps lemon juice

3 tbsps honey

Sea salt

Ground black pepper

METHOD

1. Place olive oil, lemon juice and honey in a jar with a sealable lid. Shake vigorously to combine.

2. Season to taste with salt and pepper.

SUMMER SUPER SALAD

INGREDIENTS

Salad

Large handful rocket

1 small mango, peeled and diced

1 fig, sliced

1 cup (125g, 4oz) mixed berries (blackberries and raspberries)

1-2 slices prosciutto crudo, roughly torn (optional)

¼ cup (30g, 1oz) raw pine nuts

125g (4oz) raw goat's cheese (see recipe page 8)

6-8 mint leaves

Balsamic dressing

2 tbsps honey

¼ cup (60ml, 2fl oz) balsamic vinegar

1 tbsp Dijon mustard

½ tsp sea salt

½ tsp freshly ground black pepper

1 garlic clove, minced

¾ cup (185ml, 6fl oz) extra virgin olive oil

METHOD

1. Prepare the salad ingredients and place in a serving dish.

2. In a small mixing bowl, whisk together the honey, vinegar, mustard, salt, pepper and garlic. Gradually add the oil and whisk until the dressing is fully emulsified.

3. Dress the salad and serve immediately.

FRESH CARROT SALAD

INGREDIENTS

Handful mixed salad leaves

2 carrots, peeled

1 apple, peeled

½ cup (50g, 2oz) fresh cranberries

1 tbsp black sesame seeds

Salt and pepper, to serve

METHOD

1. Using a mandolin or very sharp knife, julienne the carrot and apple.

2. Place all the ingredients in a bowl and toss to combine.

3. Transfer to serving plates and finish with fresh pepper and salt to serve.

SPICY CARROT SALAD

INGREDIENTS

8 carrots

4 cloves garlic, minced

2 tbsps ground coriander

4 tbsps vegetable oil

3 tbsps white vinegar

1 tsp salt

1 tsp cayenne pepper

1 tbsp honey

Micro greens, to garnish

METHOD

1. Prepare the carrots using a spiraliser to form long, thin strands.

2. Place all the ingredients in a large mixing bowl and thoroughly combine using your hands or a wooden spoon. Season to taste.

3. Cover with plastic wrap and transfer to the refrigerator to chill for 5 hours, before serving garnished with the micro greens.

CITRUS MARINATED BEETROOT SALAD

INGREDIENTS

1 large beetroot

Marinade

¼ cup (60ml, 2fl oz) orange juice

2 tbsps olive oil

1 tbsp balsamic vinegar

½ tsp sea salt

Salad

1 orange, peeled and cut into chunks

Large handful rocket leaves

1 tbsp sesame seeds

METHOD

1. Cut the beetroot in half from top to bottom. Place the cut side down and use a very sharp knife to cut into thin half rounds.

2. Whisk together the ingredients for the marinade and pour over the beetroot. Cover and transfer to the refrigerator to marinate overnight.

3. Remove beetroot from the refrigerator 30 minutes before serving. Drain, reserving the marinade, and bring to room temperature.

4. Arrange the salad on plates and dress with the reserved marinade.

5. Sprinkle with sesame seeds to serve.

FIG AND BERRY SALAD WITH BALSAMIC DRESSING

INGREDIENTS

Handful mixed lettuce leaves

2 figs, cut into wedges

½ cup (50g, 2oz) blueberries

½ cup (50g, 2oz) black grapes

¼ cup (25g, 1oz) pomegranate seeds

Goat's cheese (see recipe page 8)

Balsamic dressing (see recipe page 92)

METHOD

1. Arrange the salad ingredients on a plate.

2. Drizzle over the balsamic dressing.

3. Serve immediately.

CAPRESE SALAD WITH MOZZARELLA

INGREDIENTS

1 ball of vegan mozzarella (store bought or see recipe page 22), thickly sliced

2 beef tomatoes, thickly sliced

Handful of mini basil leaves

Balsamic dressing (see recipe page 92)

METHOD

1. Alternate the mozzarella and tomato slices in rows on a serving plate.

2. Scatter with basil leaves and drizzle over the balsamic dressing.

3. Serve immediately.

SUPERFOOD SALAD

INGREDIENTS

Chia seed dressing

½ lemon, juiced

¼ tsp salt

¼ tsp freshly ground pepper

1 tsp agave nectar

1 tbsp chia seeds

2 tbsps extra virgin olive oil

Salad

Handful kale leaves

Handful mixed lettuce leaves

¼ small red cabbage, chopped

1 Lebanese cucumber, chopped

1 mandarin, segmented

6 cherry tomatoes (red and yellow)

2 tbsps raw sliced almonds

½ yellow capsicum, seeded and sliced

½ green capsicum, seeded and sliced

½ cup (90g, 3oz) edamame

METHOD

1. In a small mixing bowl, whisk together the lemon, salt, pepper, agave and chia seeds. Gradually add the oil and whisk until the dressing is fully emulsified.

2. Place all the salad ingredients in a large bowl and pour over the dressing. Toss to combine.

3. Transfer to plates and serve immediately.

CREAMY CAESAR DRESSING

INGREDIENTS

2 avocados, pitted and peeled

½ cup (125ml, 4fl oz) water

¼ cup (30g, 1oz) raw cashews

¼ cup (60ml, 2fl oz) lemon juice

⅓ cup (80ml, 3fl oz) olive oil

3 tbsps apple cider vinegar

2 tbsps nutritional yeast

2-3 stems basil, leaves picked

1 tsp sea salt

¼ tsp freshly ground black pepper

2 cloves garlic

1 date, pitted

METHOD

1. Place all the ingredients in a high-speed blender and process until smooth.

2. Add more water to thin the dressing if required.

3. Taste and season with salt and pepper.

PINK DAIKON SALAD

INGREDIENTS

Salad

1 koshin (pink daikon)

1 green apple

¼ cup (10g, ¼ oz) parsley, chopped

Sesame dressing

3 tbsps rice vinegar

1 tsp sugar

1 tsp ginger, finely grated

1 tsp toasted sesame oil

¼ cup (60ml, 2fl oz) vegetable oil

METHOD

1. Peel and finely grate the daikon and apple. Transfer to serving bowl.

2. Add chopped parsley to serving bowl.

3. In a small bowl, combine the rice vinegar, sugar and ginger. Gradually whisk in the sesame oil and vegetable oil.

4. Pour dressing over the daikon and toss to combine well.

SWEDISH PICKLED FISH

INGREDIENTS

8 salted herring fillets

Pickling liquid

2 cups (500ml, 1pt)
white vinegar

¾ cup (165g, 6oz) sugar

2 bay leaves

1 carrot, roughly chopped

1 onion, sliced

2 tsps whole black
peppercorns

1 tsp yellow mustard
seeds

Salad

1-2 beetroots, very
thinly sliced

1-2 golden beetroots,
very thinly sliced

4 radishes, very thinly
sliced

220g (8oz) fresh peas

¼ cup (10g, ¼ oz)
fresh mint leaves

¼ cup (10g, ¼ oz)
fresh dill sprigs

METHOD

1. Rinse the herring fillets and place in a bowl. Cover with water and transfer to the refrigerator to soak overnight.

2. Combine all the ingredients for the pickling liquid in a medium saucepan and bring to a boil over medium-high heat. Reduce heat and simmer for 5 minutes, or until the sugar has dissolved. Remove from heat and set aside to cool to room temperature.

3. Drain the herring fillets and place in a stainless steel, ceramic or glass bowl. Pour in the cooled pickling liquid and stir to combine. Cover and set aside in a cool place to marinate for 2 days.

4. When ready to serve, remove the fillets from the pickling liquid and pat dry. Cut the fillets into small pieces.

5. Arrange the salad vegetables on a plate. Finish with the pickled fish.

ROCKMELON AND GOAT'S CHEESE SALAD

INGREDIENTS

¼ rockmelon, seeded

6 slices prosciutto crudo

Handful rocket leaves

¼ cup (30g, 1oz) raw walnuts

200g (7oz) goat's cheese (see recipe page 8)

METHOD

1. Cut the rockmelon into slim wedges.

2. Arrange the rockmelon, prosciutto, rocket leaves and walnuts among serving plates. Top with goat's cheese.

SERVES 2 ★ PREP 15MIN

PICKLED RADISH AND PEA SALAD

INGREDIENTS

1 cup (160g, 6oz) fresh shelling peas

1 small butter lettuce

½ cup (30g, 1oz) sliced pickled radish (see recipe page 116)

Lemon and honey dressing (see recipe page 91)

METHOD

1. Shell the peas by breaking the stem end and pulling the string down along the pod. Pop out the fresh peas and add to salad bowl.

2. Tear lettuce into bite-sized pieces and add to salad bowl.

3. Add radish to salad bowl.

4. Pour over the dressing and toss well to combine.

5. Transfer to plates and serve immediately.

ADZUKI SPROUT SALAD WITH LIME DRESSING

INGREDIENTS

Salad

Handful adzuki bean sprouts

Handful water spinach sprouts

1 corn cob, kernels removed

¼ white onion, sliced

½ red capsicum, finely sliced

1 tbsp black sesame seeds

Lime dressing

¼ tsp sea salt

1 tsp garlic, finely chopped

1 lime, juiced

½ cup (125ml, 4fl oz) extra virgin olive oil

1 tsp freshly ground black pepper

METHOD

1. Prepare the salad ingredients and place in a large bowl.

2. In a small bowl or jar combine the salt, garlic and lime juice. Slowly whisk in the oil until emulsified. Season with pepper to taste.

3. Pour dressing over salad and toss to combine.

DILL CUCUMBER COLESLAW

INGREDIENTS

1 small head cabbage

½ cucumber

3 tbsps dill, chopped

Dressing

1 tbsp sugar

1 tbsp sea salt

¼ cup (60ml, 2fl oz) white wine vinegar

¼ cup (60ml, 2fl oz) water

METHOD

1. Using a mandolin, sharp knife or box grater, cut the cabbage and cucumber into thin slices. Transfer to a salad bowl with the dill.

2. Dissolve the sugar and salt in the vinegar in a small bowl. Add the water and stir to combine.

3. Pour dressing over the cabbage and cucumber and toss well to combine.

4. Cover and set aside for an hour before serving.

HONEY MUSTARD DRESSING

INGREDIENTS

½ cup (60g, 2oz) raw cashews

¼ cup (60ml, 2fl oz) Dijon mustard

3 tbsps raw honey

½ tsp horseradish

¼ cup (60ml, 2fl oz) water

¼ tsp sea salt

1 tbsp chopped fresh herbs

METHOD

1. Place the cashews in a small jar and cover with water. Set aside to soak overnight.

2. Drain cashews and place in a high-speed blender. Process until smooth.

3. Add the rest of the ingredients and process until smooth.

FERMENTED FOODS AND PICKLES

THYME PRESERVED LEMONS

INGREDIENTS

4 lemons

6 tbsps coarse salt

4-5 sprigs thyme

4 peppercorns

4 lemons, juiced

METHOD

1. Wash the outside of the lemons thoroughly.

2. Place 2 tablespoons of salt in the base of the canning jar.

3. Almost cut the lemons into quarters, leaving them attached at one end.

4. Open a lemon and pour in 1 tablespoon of salt. Close the lemon and place into the jar.

5. Repeat this process until all the lemons are in the jar, squashing them down to fit. Add the thyme leaves and peppercorns. Squeeze over the juice from the additional 4 lemons so that the lemons are completely covered in liquid.

6. Close the jar tightly and store at room temperature for 3-4 weeks until the rind is soft to bite into. Shake the jar every day.

7. Transfer to the refrigerator when ready.

8. Rinse before using.

CHILLI PICKLED RADISH

INGREDIENTS

10-12 whole baby radishes

1 red chilli, sliced

1 tsp black peppercorns

¼ cup (60ml, 2fl oz)
Japanese rice vinegar

¼ cup (55g, 2oz) sugar

1 tsp salt

METHOD

1. Wash and trim the radishes.

2. Place radishes, chilli slices and black peppercorns in a clean and dry glass jar with a tight-fitting lid.

3. Mix vinegar, sugar and salt together in a bowl and stir to combine. Pour liquid over the radishes.

4. Secure the lid and gently shake or upend the jar until sugar and salt begin to dissolve.

5. Refrigerate for at least 3 days, shaking once a day, and then pickles are ready to eat.

EASY PICKLED TOMATOES

INGREDIENTS

2 punnets cherry tomatoes

4-6 cloves garlic, thinly sliced

1 carrot, peeled and cubed

2 bay leaves

1 tsp caraway seeds

2 tbsps sea salt

2 cups (500ml, 1pt) water

1 tbsp lime juice

METHOD

1. Place tomatoes, garlic, carrots, bay leaves and caraway seeds into glass jars until three-quarters full.

2. Create a brine solution by dissolving salt and water. Add lime juice.

3. Pour the liquid into the jars, completely covering the tomatoes and herbs. Add more brine if necessary.

4. Secure with a tight-fitting lid and allow to ferment at room temperature for 7 days.

5. Refrigerate after first use.

SERVES 6 CUPS ★ PREP 30MIN (PLUS FERMENTING)

KIMCHI

INGREDIENTS

1 head Chinese cabbage

1 daikon, chopped

2 tbsps coarse salt

8 spring onions, white part only, chopped

8 cloves garlic

Medium piece ginger, peeled and roughly chopped

½ cup (50g, 2oz) Korean chilli powder (gochukaru)

2 tbsps white miso paste

1 tbsp sugar

1 cup (250ml, 8fl oz) water

METHOD

1. To prepare the cabbage, pull off leaves and discard the central core.

2. Place cabbage leaves and daikon in a large bowl and sprinkle salt over. Toss to combine. Cover and allow to sit at room temperature for a minimum of 1 hour and overnight if possible. When ready, cabbage leaves will be soft and around ½ cup (125ml, 4fl oz) of liquid released.

3. Meanwhile, combine spring onion, garlic, ginger, chilli powder, miso paste and sugar in the bowl of a food processor or blender. Process for up to 1 minute until a rough paste forms.

4. Pour chilli mixture over the cabbage. Add water and toss to coat well. Taste and add more salt if required.

5. Pack the cabbage mixture into glass jars, pressing down firmly to remove any air trapped in the jar. Pour in soaking liquid to completely cover the cabbage and then seal the jars tightly.

6. Allow jars to sit at room temperature for 24 hours and then transfer to the fridge to ferment for 1 week before eating.

SERVES 3 CUPS ★ PREP 20MIN (PLUS PICKLING)

PICKLED RED CABBAGE

INGREDIENTS

½ small head red cabbage

1 cup (250ml, 8fl oz) water

½ cup (125ml, 4fl oz) apple cider vinegar

½ cup (125ml, 4fl oz) red wine vinegar

2 tsps light brown sugar

2 cloves garlic, crushed

2 bay leaves

1 tsp salt

¼ tsp black pepper

METHOD

1. Using a mandolin or very sharp knife, shred the cabbage, discarding the core. Transfer to a large sealable container.

2. In a separate bowl, whisk together the water, two types of vinegar and sugar. Stir until sugar has dissolved. Add the garlic, bay leaves, salt and pepper and stir.

3. Pour mixture over the cabbage and then seal the container and set aside to marinate for 3 hours at room temperature. Transfer to the fridge to chill for at least 1 hour before serving.

4. Stir and serve.

DO CHUA (VIETNAMESE DAIKON PICKLES)

INGREDIENTS

2 daikon, peeled

4 cups (1L, 2pt) warm water

⅓ cup (80ml, 3fl oz) white vinegar or rice vinegar

3 tbsps sugar

2 tbsps sea salt

2 tbsps coriander seeds

METHOD

1. Using a mandolin or very sharp knife, cut daikon into small matchsticks.

2. Combine water, vinegar, sugar and salt in a large bowl and stir gently until dissolved.

3. Place daikon and coriander seeds in a dry glass jar and cover with the liquid, leaving a gap of around 2cm (1in) below the lid.

4. Close with a tight-fitting lid and transfer to the refrigerator for at least 24 hours before serving.

SAUERKRAUT

INGREDIENTS

1 white cabbage

3 carrots, peeled and grated

3 tsps fine sea salt

1 tbsp ginger, grated

2 cloves garlic, finely chopped

1 cup (250ml, 8fl oz) brine (1 tbsp of sea salt dissolved in 1 cup water)

METHOD

1. Using a mandolin or box grater, separately shred the cabbage and carrot. Set carrot aside.

2. Transfer the cabbage to a large glass or ceramic bowl and sprinkle with sea salt. Mix to coat the cabbage and set aside for 10 minutes.

3. Next, using hands or a potato masher, squeeze the cabbage for 10 minutes to release all the natural moisture. Add carrot and toss to combine.

4. Pack the vegetables, ginger and garlic into a glass jar tightly to remove as many air pockets as possible.

5. Pour in the brine ensuring that vegetables are covered with about 2cm (1in) of water on top. If there is insufficient brine, add more water and salt in the same ratio.

6. Place a cheesecloth over the vegetables and secure it with a weighted object, such as a water-filled jar or heavy stone. Press down firmly to remove any remaining air pockets.

7. Cover the fermenting jar with a clean and dry tea towel and place it on a plate to capture any spillage.

8. Place the container in a dry place at room temperature and out of direct sunlight and leave to ferment for 5-7 days. Check daily to ensure the liquid still covers the vegetables.

9. Transfer to a glass jar and store in the fridge when ready.

RAW BREAD AND BUTTER PICKLES

INGREDIENTS

2 Continental cucumbers, sliced

2-3 garlic cloves, peeled and sliced

3 tbsps dill, finely chopped

2 tbsps mini basil leaves

1 cup (250ml, 8fl oz) apple cider vinegar

½ cup (125ml, 4fl oz) water

½ cup (180g, 6oz) raw agave syrup

2 tbsps brown rice vinegar

1 tbsp mixed peppercorns

METHOD

1. Toss cucumber, garlic, dill and mini basil leaves together.

2. Pack into two glass jars.

3. In a small bowl, combine the apple cider vinegar, water, agave, brown rice vinegar and peppercorns. Whisk to combine.

4. Pour the liquid over the cucumbers and secure the jars with a tight-fitting lid.

5. Place in the refrigerator for 24 hours before eating.

PICKLED PINK CAULIFLOWER

INGREDIENTS

1 head cauliflower, cut into florets

1 beetroot, peeled and sliced

4 cloves garlic, thinly sliced

3 cups (750ml, 24fl oz) water

½ cup (125ml, 4fl oz) white vinegar

¼ cup (55g, 2oz) salt

Pinch of chilli flakes

4-6 black peppercorns (optional)

METHOD

1. Pack the vegetables and garlic into one or two clean and dry glass jars with tight-fitting lids.

2. Place the water in a saucepan over medium-high heat. Add the vinegar, salt, chilli flakes and peppercorns and bring to the boil. Stir well until salt has fully dissolved then set aside to cool.

3. Pour cooled liquid over the vegetables and close the lid tightly.

4. Set aside at room temperature for 48 hours.

5. Refrigerate after opening.

FERMENTED RED ONION

INGREDIENTS

2 red onions, sliced into rings

1 cup (250ml, 8fl oz) brine (1 tbsp of sea salt dissolved in 1 cup of filtered water)

METHOD

1. Pack sliced onions firmly into a glass jar.

2. Pour in the brine ensuring that onions are covered with about 2cm (1in) of water on top. If there is insufficient brine, add more water and salt in the same ratio. Use a weight to keep the onions under the brine, if necessary. Seal with a lid.

3. Place the jar in a dry place at room temperature for 5-7 days. Loosen the lid each day to release gases and then close firmly.

4. Store in the fridge when ready.

PICKLES WITH GARLIC AND CHILLI

INGREDIENTS

5-6 pickling cucumbers

1 tbsp mustard seeds

2 tbsps sea salt

3 cloves garlic, sliced

2 long red chilli peppers, seeded and chopped

1 cup (250ml, 8fl oz) water

METHOD

1. Wash cucumbers well and place in a wide-mouthed glass jar with a tight-fitting lid.

2. Combine remaining ingredients and pour over cucumbers, adding more water if necessary to cover the cucumbers, leaving a gap of around 2cm (1in) below the lid.

3. Secure the lid and allow to sit at room temperature for 3 days before transferring to the refrigerator.

FERMENTED EGGPLANT

INGREDIENTS

2 medium eggplants, diced

Salt, for sprinkling

2 tbsps sea salt

4 cups (1L, 2pts) water

6 cloves garlic, crushed

2 tsps fresh oregano, chopped

2 tbsps fresh basil, chopped

METHOD

1. Place eggplant pieces in a colander set over a dish and sprinkle generously with salt. Massage the salt into the eggplant. Cover with a clean tea towel and set aside for 1 hour. Rinse and pat dry with kitchen paper.

2. Meanwhile, heat the sea salt and water in a saucepan over medium-high heat until completely dissolved. Set aside to cool to room temperature.

3. Place garlic and fresh herbs in a glass jar. Add eggplant pieces, pushing them in firmly. Pour in the brine so that it completely covers the eggplant and rises above by about 2cm (1in). Seal with a lid.

4. Place jar in a dry place at room temperature for 5-7 days. Loosen the lid each day to release gases and then close firmly.

5. Store in the refrigerator when ready to eat.

PICKLED MUSHROOMS

INGREDIENTS

225g (8oz, ½ lb) button mushrooms

3 tbsps olive oil

2 tbsps lemon juice

2 tsps soy sauce

1 tbsp maple syrup

1 tsp black peppercorns

METHOD

1. Wash and dry mushrooms. Place in a glass jar or plastic container.

2. Whisk together the oil, lemon juice, soy sauce, maple syrup and peppercorns.

3. Pour the marinade over the mushrooms and toss to fully coat.

4. Refrigerate for 4 hours, stirring every hour.

TSUKEMONO

INGREDIENTS

1 small head white cabbage

2 tbsps sea salt

1 daikon, grated

1 tsp caraway seeds (optional)

4 cups (1L, 2pt) water

1 piece dashi kombu, about 5 x 10cm (2 x 4in)

METHOD

1. Using a mandolin or box grater, finely shred the cabbage.

2. Transfer the cabbage to a large glass or ceramic bowl and sprinkle with the sea salt. Mix to coat the cabbage and set aside for 10 minutes.

3. Next, using hands or a potato masher, squeeze the cabbage for 10 minutes to release all the natural moisture.

4. Add the daikon and caraway seeds, if using, and stir to combine.

5. Add water to cover the cabbage by about 2cm (1in). If there is insufficient water, add more water and salt in the 2 tablespoons to 4 cups (1L, 2pt) ratio.

6. Place the dashi kombu on top of the cabbage.

7. Place a cheesecloth over the cabbage and secure it with a weighted object, such as a water-filled jar or heavy stone. Press down firmly to remove any air pockets.

8. Place the bowl in a dry place at room temperature and out of direct sunlight and leave to ferment for 5-7 days. Check daily to ensure the liquid still covers the cabbage.

9. Transfer to a glass jar and store in the fridge when ready.

QUICK PICKLED ASPARAGUS

INGREDIENTS

700g (1½ lb) asparagus

1 small red onion, cut into wedges

1 cup (250ml, 8fl oz) water

½ cup (110g, 4oz) sugar

1½ cups (375ml, 13fl oz) white wine vinegar

2 tbsps salt

4 cloves garlic, sliced thinly

2 tbsps yellow mustard seeds

2-3 sprigs thyme

METHOD

1. Wash and dry the asparagus and trim off the tough bottom part of the stems.

2. Arrange the asparagus vertically in a large, clean and dry glass jar. Squeeze the onion and thyme in around the asparagus.

3. Combine all the other ingredients in a saucepan over a medium-high heat and bring the mixture to a boil. Set aside to cool slightly then pour the liquid into the jar.

4. Seal with a tight-fitting lid and then leave to cool at room temperature for up to 3 days until asparagus is tender.

5. Refrigerate after opening.

HERBY PICKLED ZUCCHINI

INGREDIENTS

3 cloves garlic, halved

2-3 bay leaves

6-8 peppercorns

4 zucchini, sliced into half moons

¼ cup (10g, ¼ oz) fresh parsley, chopped

¼ cup (10g, ¼ oz) fresh dill, chopped

1 tbsp chives, finely chopped

1-2 sprigs rosemary

1 tbsp coriander seeds

3 cups (750ml, 24fl oz) boiling hot water

2 tbsps olive oil

½ cup (125ml, 4fl oz) white vinegar

⅓ cup (70g, 2½ oz) white sugar

1 tbsp sea salt

METHOD

1. Place garlic, bay leaves and peppercorns into the bottom of a clean and dry glass jar with a tight-fitting lid

2. Pack jar tightly with zucchini, herbs and coriander seeds.

3. Combine hot water, olive oil, vinegar, sugar and salt and stir until sugar and salt have dissolved. Allow to cool slightly, then pour over the zucchini.

4. Seal jar with the lid and set aside at room temperature for 24 hours before using.

5. Refrigerate after opening.

SERVES 6 ★ PREP 30MIN (PLUS PICKLING)

MANGO PICKLE

INGREDIENTS

4 cups (165g, 6oz) unripe firm mango, peeled

2 tbsps salt

¼ cup (55g, 2oz) salt

1 tbsp mustard seeds

1 tbsp fenugreek seeds

3 tbsps chilli powder

4 cloves garlic

1 tbsp nigella seeds (optional)

1 tbsp fennel seeds

1 tbsp coriander seeds

½ cup (125ml, 4fl oz) peanut oil

METHOD

1. Place mango in a bowl and cover with 2 tablespoons of salt. Gently rub salt into the mango flesh. Cover and set aside for 8-12 hours. Drain liquid from the mango and pat dry with kitchen paper. Cut into chunks and discard stone.

2. Using a pestle and mortar or a spice grinder, pound the spices and garlic until roughly ground and aromatic.

3. Ensure that glass jars are very dry before use. Place mango, salt and spices in glass jars.

4. Pour in the oil and secure with a lid. Turn a few times to mix.

5. Set aside for 24 hours before eating.

    Note: Flavour develops over 3-4 weeks and a soft texture after months of marination. Store in the fridge after opening.

★

LIGHT MEALS

★

RAW PIZZA WITH BASIL PESTO

INGREDIENTS

Crust

¼ cup (40g, 1½ oz) hemp seeds

¼ cup (30g, 1oz) pumpkin seeds

¼ cup (30g, 1oz) sunflower seeds

1 cup (125g, 4oz) raw almonds

¾ cup (90g, 3oz) walnuts

Handful fresh basil

¼ tsp sea salt

¼ tsp fresh pepper

1-2 tbsps water, as needed

Toppings

1 cup (225g, 8oz) basil pesto (see recipe page 29)

½ red onion, sliced (or use fermented red onion, see page 127)

5-6 cherry tomatoes

Handful black olives, sliced

¼ cup (30g, 1oz) raw pine nuts

Handful fresh basil leaves

METHOD

1. Turn on the oven to the lowest possible temperature or make ready your dehydrator. Line two baking trays with greaseproof paper or prepare dehydrator trays.

2. Place all the dry ingredients for the pizza crust in a food processor or blender and process until the mixture sticks together. Add a little water if necessary.

3. Form into two dough balls and then flatten slightly. Press the mixture onto prepared trays into desired size.

4. Transfer to the oven or dehydrator and cook for 5 hours or until dry and crispy.

5. Meanwhile, prepare the vegetables and basil pesto.

6. When crusts are ready, assemble the pizzas by spreading with a layer of basil pesto and arranging vegetables, pine nuts and herbs on top.

ZOODLES WITH PISTACHIO PESTO

INGREDIENTS

4 zucchinis

Pistachio pesto

½ cup (60g, 2oz) raw shelled pistachios

2 sprigs fresh basil

1 cup (30g, 1oz) spinach

1 clove garlic

1 lemon, juiced

¼ cup (60ml, 2fl oz) extra virgin olive oil

8-10 cherry tomatoes, halved

METHOD

1. Wash the zucchinis. Use a spiral slicer, julienne peeler or very sharp knife to slice the zucchini into noodles. Place zoodles into serving bowls.

2. To make the pesto, place the ingredients in a high-speed blender or food processor and process until the desired consistency is reached. Add extra oil or lemon juice for a looser and smoother consistency.

3. Spoon pesto on top of zoodles and garnish with cherry tomato halves to serve.

VEGAN ROLLS WITH SPROUTED GREENS

INGREDIENTS

4 rice paper wrappers

Kale pesto (see recipe page 38)

2 tbsps black sesame seeds

1 carrot, peeled and julienned

1 green capsicum, seeded and finely sliced

1 Lebanese cucumber, finely sliced

½ cup (20g, ¾ oz) mint, chopped

½ avocado, peeled, stoned and cut into slices

Large handful spicy salad sprouts

METHOD

1. Prepare a bowl of warm water and a clean tea towel. Spread the tea towel on a clean workbench. Sprinkle a quarter of the black sesame seeds onto the tea towel.

2. Fully immerse a rice paper sheet into the water for 10 seconds or until just soft. Remove and place on the tea towel.

3. Spread thin layer of pesto over rice paper wrapper.

4. Place vegetable filling at the bottom edge of the rice paper wrapper and fold the sides inward. Tightly roll from the bottom up.

5. Slice each roll with a very sharp knife to serve.

6. Repeat with the remaining rice paper wrappers.

STUFFED MUSHROOMS WITH WASABI MAYONNAISE

INGREDIENTS

6 large button mushrooms

Marinade

¼ cup (60ml, 2fl oz) sesame oil

1 tbsp tamari

1 lime, juiced

Stuffing

¾ cup (120g, 4oz) hemp seeds

1 carrot, chopped

2 tbsps coriander, packed

1 clove garlic, chopped

1 tsp cumin

1 lime, juiced

¼ cup (60ml, 2fl oz) sesame oil

2 tbsps tamari

Wasabi mayonnaise

2 cups (250g, 8oz) cashews, soaked for 30 minutes

1½ cups (375ml, 13fl oz) water

1 clove garlic, minced

2 tbsps lemon juice

3 tbsps wasabi paste

¼ tsp sea salt

1 tbsp extra virgin olive oil

1 tbsp apple cider vinegar

METHOD

1. Clean and dry the mushrooms with paper towel. Remove and discard stalks.

2. To make the marinade, place all the ingredients in a small bowl and whisk together.

3. Pour marinade into a flat dish and place mushrooms on top. Set aside to marinate for 1 hour.

4. To make the stuffing place all of the ingredients in a food processor or high-speed blender and process until smooth but still retaining some texture.

5. To make the wasabi mayonnaise, blend all ingredients in a high-speed blender until smooth.

6. Spoon stuffing into the mushrooms and top with wasabi mayonnaise.

OKROSHKA (COLD KEFIR SOUP)

INGREDIENTS

2 spring onions, finely chopped

¼ cup (10g, ¼ oz) finely chopped dill

1 small bunch radishes, cut in half and thinly sliced

4 Lebanese cucumbers, diced

½ green capsicum, seeded and diced

3 cups (750ml, 24fl oz) raw milk or coconut milk kefir

2 tbsps apple cider vinegar

1½ cups (375ml, 13fl oz) water

2 cups (500ml, 1pt) sparkling water

Sea salt and freshly cracked pepper, to taste

Fresh dill and chopped chives, to garnish

METHOD

1. Place the spring onions, dill, radishes, cucumber and capsicum in a large bowl.

2. In a separate bowl, combine kefir, vinegar and still and sparkling water until the desired consistency and fizz is achieved.

3. Pour the kefir-water mixture over the vegetables and season to taste with salt and pepper.

4. Serve garnished with fresh dill and chives.

BEETROOT CARPACCIO WITH RASPBERRY DRESSING

INGREDIENTS

2 large beetroots

2 tsps virgin olive oil

1 tsp raw apple cider vinegar

Raspberry dressing

1 tsp Dijon mustard

1 tsp honey

2 tbsps good quality balsamic vinegar

1 tsp raspberry vinegar

3 tbsps extra virgin olive oil

To serve

2 tbsps pine nuts

Small handful salad leaves

METHOD

1. Wash and peel the beetroots. Using a sharp knife or a mandolin cut into very thin slices.

2. Combine the olive oil and apple cider vinegar in a small bowl. Pour mixture over the beetroot to keep it moist and glossy.

3. Arrange beetroot in concentric circles on plates.

4. To make the dressing, place the mustard and honey in a small bowl and blend with a whisk. Add vinegars and stir to combine. Gradually add olive oil, stirring until it emulsifies.

5. Drizzle dressing over beetroot, then finish with garnish of pine nuts and salad leaves.

BEETROOT GAZPACHO

INGREDIENTS

4 sun-dried tomato halves

2 medium stalks celery

2 small cucumbers, roughly chopped

4 beetroots, roughly chopped

2 large tomatoes, roughly chopped

½ tsp sea salt

2 Medjool dates (pitted)

5 basil leaves

¼ cup (60ml, 2fl oz) olive oil

1 tbsp apple cider vinegar

Pinch red chilli flakes

½ cup (125ml, 4fl oz) soaking water (from the tomatoes)

1 cup (250ml, 8fl oz) vegetable stock or water

1 cup (150g, 5oz) ice cubes

METHOD

1. Rehydrate the sun-dried tomatoes by placing them in a bowl and covering with water. Set aside for 3 hours. Drain and retain the draining liquid.

2. Blend all ingredients in a high-speed blender until fully combined and smooth and with required degree of warmth from the blender.

3. Serve garnished with chopped cucumber and radish pieces.

HAWAIIAN AHI POKE

INGREDIENTS

350g (12oz) raw sashimi-grade tuna, cut into 2cm (1in) cubes

1 tsp white sesame seeds

4 tsps tamari

2 tsps sesame oil

1 tsp honey

Pinch sea salt

To serve

2 tbsps white sesame seed powder

Handful micro greens

1 tbsp black sesame seeds

1 tbsp white sesame seeds

METHOD

1. Place the tuna in a bowl and add sesame seeds, tamari, sesame oil, honey and salt. Turn gently to coat the fish. Taste and adjust seasonings as required.

2. Allow to sit at room temperature for 5-10 minutes before serving.

3. Serve garnished with micro greens and powdered sesame seed.

SERVES 4 ★ PREP 20MIN
BEEF TARTARE

INGREDIENTS

2 tsps brined capers, drained and rinsed

3 tsps Dijon mustard

2 large egg yolks

300g (10oz) prime beef tenderloin, cut into small pieces, chilled

1 tsp fresh black pepper

¼ onion, finely diced

4 tsps olive oil

3 drops hot sauce

4 drops Worcestershire sauce

METHOD

1. Place capers, mustard and egg in a glass or ceramic bowl. Using a fork whisk ingredients together until evenly combined.

2. Using a rubber spatula fold remaining ingredients into mustard mixture until thoroughly combined.

3. Season well with salt and freshly ground black pepper.

4. Serve immediately.

SERVES 2 ★ PREP 15MIN

LETTUCE WRAPS WITH SATAY SAUCE

INGREDIENTS

Satay sauce

½ cup (65g, 2oz) peanut butter

2 tbsps tamari

2 tbsps sesame oil

1 lime, juiced and zested

1 tbsp coconut sugar

1 tbsp garlic, finely chopped

1 tbsp ginger, grated

½ tsp crushed red pepper flakes

Wraps

4 large butter lettuce leaves, washed and dried

½ red capsicum, seeded and finely sliced into strips

1 yellow capsicum, seeded and finely sliced into strips

1 carrot, peeled and finely sliced into strips

½ zucchini, cut lengthwise and finely sliced into strips

To serve

Sprinkle of chopped raw peanuts

Few sprigs flat-leaf parsley

METHOD

1. Put the ingredients for the satay sauce into a high-speed blender and process until smooth, stopping to scrape down the sides once or twice as needed.

2. Open lettuce leaves flat on a clean surface. Place a quarter of the vegetables horizontally at the bottom of one leaf and roll over to create a wrap. Repeat with the remaining leaves and vegetables.

3. Serve with satay sauce and extra peanuts and parsley, to garnish.

CHILEAN CEVICHE

INGREDIENTS

1kg (2lb) firm-fleshed fish, cut into small pieces

½ red onion, finely diced

1 green serrano chilli, seeded and finely diced

2 tsps sea salt

¼ cup (10g, ¼ oz) parsley, finely chopped

½ cup (125ml, 4fl oz) lime juice

½ cup (125ml, 4fl oz) lemon juice

METHOD

1. Place the fish in a ceramic or glass dish.

2. Sprinkle over the onion, chilli, salt and parsley.

3. Pour over the lime and lemon juice.

4. Cover the dish with plastic wrap and transfer to the refrigerator for 1 hour.

5. Remove and stir well to ensure fish is coated with juices on all sides.

6. Return to the refrigerator for a further 3 hours before serving.

CARROT SUSHI

INGREDIENTS

4 carrots, peeled and roughly chopped

2 tsps apple cider vinegar

2 nori seaweed sheets

½ avocado, peeled, stoned and cut into strips

½ red capsicum, seeded and sliced into strips

1 yellow capsicum, seeded and sliced into strips

⅓ kohlrabi, peeled and sliced into strips

1 stem Thai basil, leaves picked

METHOD

1. Place the carrots in a food processor and process until a rice-like consistency forms. Add the vinegar and process again until combined.

2. Lay the nori sheets shiny side down on a clean surface and spread the carrot rice mixture onto each sheet until it reaches the edges, leaving a border at the top and bottom.

3. Place the vegetables and basil at the bottom of the sheet on top of the rice.

4. Roll from the bottom, using thumbs to roll and fingers to keep the vegetables intact. Apply even and firm pressure.

5. Dab water or lemon juice at the top of the nori roll to create a seal at one end.

6. Cut into slices using a very sharp knife.

   Note: Use a bamboo mat to roll the sushi if you have one.

VEGETABLE AND COCONUT BURRITO

INGREDIENTS

Wraps

½ cup (60g, 2oz) linseed

½ tsp sea salt

3 red capsicums, seeded

1 zucchini, peeled

1 cup (55g, 2oz) sun-dried tomatoes

½ avocado

1½ tbsps chia seeds

Coconut filling

1 zucchini

1 cup (200g, 7oz) raw coconut meat

1 ripe avocado

½ tsp ground cumin

½ tsp ground coriander

2 cloves garlic

1 celery rib, chopped

Handful of fresh coriander

½ cup (60g, 2oz) linseed

2 cups (200g, 7oz) mushrooms, chopped

To serve

1 red capsicum, sliced

1 cucumber, sliced

1 carrot, peeled and sliced

METHOD

1. To make wraps, blend all ingredients together in a high-speed blender until smooth and thick. Use the tamper tool to push down as required.

2. Evenly spread layers of mixture onto dehydrator sheets.

3. Dehydrate at 45°C (115°F) for at least 6 hours or until you can peel the wrap off the sheet. When ready, flip and return to the dehydrator until the wrap is completely dry but still pliable.

4. To make the coconut filling, put all the ingredients apart from the mushrooms into a food processor. Pulse until a dip-like consistency forms. Add a little water or coconut water to thin the mixture, if needed. Transfer to a mixing bowl and stir in the mushrooms. Cover and transfer to sit in the refrigerator for at least 2 hours, until flavours are well blended.

5. To serve, pile filling and vegetables on one end and then carefully roll into a burrito.

CREAM OF MUSHROOM SOUP

INGREDIENTS

1¼ cups (105g, 4oz) button mushrooms, washed and roughly chopped

⅓ cup (40g, 1½ oz) cashews

⅓ cup (80ml, 3fl oz) water

1 tbsp fresh thyme leaves

¼ tsp sea salt

⅓ cup (35g, 1¼ oz) button mushrooms, finely sliced

Thyme leaves for garnish

METHOD

1. Place roughly chopped button mushrooms, cashews, water, thyme and sea salt in a food processor or high-speed blender and process on high for 5 minutes or until very smooth and slightly warm from the heat of the blender.

2. Transfer into serving bowls. Add remaining mushrooms into the bowls and stir gently to combine.

3. Serve garnished with mushroom slices and thyme

CORN AND DILL CHOWDER

INGREDIENTS

1 cup (170g, 6oz) fresh corn kernels

¼ cup (30g, 1oz) cashews

¾ cup (185ml, 6fl oz) water

2 tbsps olive oil

1 tbsp lemon juice

1 tbsp dill, chopped

¾ tsp sea salt

½ cup (80g, 3oz) more fresh corn kernels

METHOD

1. Place the corn kernels, cashews, water, olive oil, lemon juice, dill and sea salt in a food processor or high-speed blender and process on high for 5 minutes or until very smooth and slightly warm from the heat of the blender.

2. Transfer into serving bowls. Add remaining corn into the bowls and stir gently to combine.

3. Serve garnished with dill.

GREEN PEA HUMMUS COCKTAIL

INGREDIENTS

Green pea hummus

2 cups (340g, 12oz) fresh peas

2 tbsps raw tahini

1 tbsp olive oil

2 tbsps lemon juice

¼ tsp salt

2 tbsps fresh basil leaves, chopped

Water, as needed

To serve

6 radishes, quartered

1 carrot, peeled and julienned

2 Lebanese cucumbers, diced

1 cup (170g, 6oz) peas

Handful buckwheat lettuce or other sprouted greens

METHOD

1. To make the hummus place all ingredients in the bowl of a food processor or high-speed blender and process until smooth. Add water to achieve desired consistency.

2. Serve in glasses topped with radish, carrot, cucumber, peas and sprouted greens.

CAULIFLOWER MASH

INGREDIENTS

1 cup (125g, 4oz) raw cashews

1 medium head cauliflower (chopped)

1 clove garlic

1 tbsp olive oil

2 tbsps water

½ tsp sea salt

Pinch black pepper

METHOD

1. Place the cashews in a bowl and cover with water. Set aside to soak for one hour. Drain and rinse.

2. Place all the cauliflower in a food processor and process until crumbly with the texture of rice. Scrape down the food processor occasionally if needed.

3. Add the other ingredients and process until smooth and creamy with the texture of mashed potato.

4. Serve cold, or warm in the dehydrator at 45°C (115°F) for 1 hour or until warm.

GREEN PEA SOUP

INGREDIENTS

2 cups (500ml, 1pt) vegetable stock or water

¼ cup (30g, 1oz) raw cashews

1 clove garlic, peeled

2 cups (340g, 12oz) peas

2 cups (60g, 2oz) fresh baby spinach

1 tbsp fresh lemon juice

1 tbsp fresh rosemary, chopped

Salt and freshly ground black pepper, to taste

METHOD

1. Place the stock or water, cashews and garlic into food processor or high-speed blender and process until completely smooth.

2. Add the peas, spinach, lemon juice and rosemary and process at high speed until thick and smooth.

3. Season to taste with freshly ground black pepper, salt, and additional lemon juice, if needed.

RAW GREEN SUSHI ROLLS

INGREDIENTS

4 sheets of nori

Rice

½ head cauliflower, in florets

1 head broccoli florets

½ cup (20g, ¾ oz) parsley

1 tbsp fresh ginger, grated

¼ cup (40g, 1½ oz) hemp seeds

1 tbsp ground linseed

2 tsps apple cider vinegar

Filling

1 avocado, peeled, stoned and cut into strips

1 carrot, peeled and julienned

1 red capsicum, seeded and sliced into strips

METHOD

1. Place the cauliflower, broccoli and parsley in a food processor and process until a rice-like consistency forms.

2. Add the grated ginger, hemp seeds, linseed and apple cider vinegar to the food processor and pulse until combined.

3. Lay the nori sheet shiny side down on a clean surface and spread the rice mixture onto each sheet until it reaches the edges, but leave a border at the top and bottom.

4. Place the filling vegetables at the bottom of the sheet on top of the rice.

5. Roll from the bottom, using thumbs to roll and fingers to keep the vegetables intact. Apply even and firm pressure.

6. Dab water or lemon juice at the top of the nori roll to create a seal at one end.

7. Cut into slices using a very sharp knife.

   Note: Use a bamboo mat to roll the sushi if you have one.

BLACK BEAN PIZZA

INGREDIENTS

Crust

1 x 400g (14oz) can black beans, rinsed and drained

2 tbsps black chia seeds

2 tbsps ground linseed

1 tsp sea salt

1 cup (170g, 6oz) buckwheat, soaked

1 cup (125g, 4oz) sunflower seeds

Pinch cayenne pepper

¼ cup (60ml, 2fl oz) olive oil

2 cloves garlic

Toppings

1 cup (60g, 2oz) black beans

Fermented red onions (see recipe page 127)

8 cherry tomatoes, sliced

½ cup (80g, 3oz) corn kernels

Handful fresh spinach leaves

METHOD

1. Place all the ingredients for the crust in the bowl of a food processor and process until well combined but still with some texture.

2. Scrape the mixture out onto a lined dehydrator tray.

3. Press the mixture down and work it into a large flat circle, about 5mm (¼ in) thick. Roughly score with a sharp knife into slices.

4. Place in the dehydrator at 45°C (115°F) for 8 hours, until dry and crisp to the touch. Flip over and remove the liner. Break into individual slices and return to the dehydrator for a further 8 hours until completely dry and crunchy.

5. Arrange toppings over the pizza and serve.

AVOCADO LIME SOUP

INGREDIENTS

½ cucumber

1 avocado

1 tomato

1 cup (250ml, 8fl oz) water

2 cups (60g, 2oz) spinach

1 spring onion

½ lime, juiced

½ tsp cayenne pepper

½ sea salt

To garnish

2 tbsps raw peanuts

2 tbsps sesame seeds

3-4 basil leaves

METHOD

1. Place the cucumber, avocado, tomato, water, spinach, spring onion, lime juice, cayenne pepper and salt in a high-speed blender and process until smooth.

2. Serve garnished with peanuts, sesame seeds and basil.

SERVES 4 ★ PREP 50MIN (PLUS SOAKING, DEHYDRATING AND CHILLING)

VEGAN LASAGNE

INGREDIENTS

Lasagne sheets

2 cups (250g, 8oz) sunflower seeds

½ tsp salt

2 tsps cardamom

⅛ tsp cayenne

¼ cup (40g, 1½oz) ground linseed

¼ cup (55g, 2oz) tahini

1 orange capsicum

2 tbsps nutritional yeast

½ cup (125ml, 4fl oz) water

Bechamel

1 cup (125g, 4oz) macadamia nuts (soaked overnight)

1 cup (125g, 4oz) cashew nuts (soaked overnight)

1 cup (250ml, 8fl oz) water

¼ tsp sea salt

½ red capsicum, seeded

Vegetables

2 tomatoes, sliced

1 cup (150g, 5oz) pickled red cabbage (see page 120)

2 carrots, grated

1 green capsicum, deseeded and sliced

Hemp seeds and basil leaves

METHOD

1. Place the sunflower seeds in a high-speed blender or food processor and process until a fine flour forms.

2. Add the other ingredients for the lasagne sheets except for the water and process until combined. Gradually add water until a thick puree consistency forms.

3. Spread the dough evenly onto a dehydrator tray to form a rectangle.

4. Place in the dehydrator at 43°C (110°F) and leave for 8 hours until dry. Remove and score the lasagne sheets into desired size, then return to the dehydrator for a further 4-6 hours until completely dry but still pliable.

5. Drain and rinse the nuts, and transfer to a high-speed blender. Add water, salt and capsicum. Pulse until a paste forms.

6. Transfer the paste to a bowl. Cover and place in the refrigerator overnight to set.

7. To assemble the lasagne, alternate layers of lasagne sheets with fresh vegetables and bechamel sauce. Garnish with hemp seeds and fresh basil to serve.

TOMATO SOUP

INGREDIENTS

4-6 ripe tomatoes

3 sun-dried tomatoes

2 stalks celery

½ clove garlic, finely grated

2 sprigs basil

½ tsp sea salt

½ tsp fresh black pepper

½ ripe avocado, peeled and stoned

To serve

½ cup (125ml, 4fl oz) cashew cream (see recipe page 14)

Handful micro greens

Fresh black pepper

METHOD

1. Place the tomatoes in a high-speed blender or food processor and process until smooth.

2. With the machine still running, add the sun-dried tomatoes, celery, garlic, basil, salt and pepper and blend until thoroughly combined.

3. Add the avocado and process for 5-10 seconds.

4. Serve garnished with a swirl of cashew cream, a handful of micro greens and fresh black pepper.

SERVES 4 ★ PREP 15MIN

ZUCCHINI SOUP

INGREDIENTS

4 medium zucchinis, diced

1⅓ cups (225g, 8oz) frozen peas, thawed

2 stalks celery, roughly chopped

1 avocado, peeled and stoned

1 cup (250ml, 8fl oz) water

¼ cup (60ml, 2fl oz) fresh lemon juice

2 cloves garlic, finely grated

Sea salt and freshly ground pepper, to taste

1 tbsp fresh parsley plus extra for garnish

METHOD

1. Place the zucchini (reserving some for garnish), peas, celery, avocado, water, lemon juice, garlic, salt, pepper and parsley in a high-speed blender or food processor and process until smooth

2. Serve garnished with sliced zucchini and fresh parsley.

SALMON TARTARE ON AVOCADO

INGREDIENTS

115g (4oz) very fresh salmon fillet, skin removed

½ small cucumber, finely diced

1 tbsp capers

2 tbsps lime juice

2 tbsps flat-leaf parsley, finely chopped

2 tsps olive oil

2 ripe avocados, sliced in half, stones removed

Handful cress

Salt and pepper, to taste

METHOD

1. Carefully remove all the bones from the fish. Place salmon on a plate and cover with plastic wrap. Transfer to the freezer to chill for 20 minutes.

2. Place all of the other ingredients except the avocados in a bowl and mix together.

3. Remove salmon from the freezer and using a very sharp knife cut into small cubes.

4. Add salmon to the bowl and toss through the mix.

5. Spoon tartare into avocado halves and garnish with cress and salt and pepper.

COCONUT DILL SOUP

INGREDIENTS

1 cucumber, diced

½ cup (125ml, 4fl oz) full cream coconut milk

½ cup (125ml, 4fl oz) iced water

½ lemon, juiced

½ zucchini, finely grated

Handful mint leaves

Handful dill leaves

Salt and pepper, to taste

¼ cup (30g, 1oz) raw walnuts, chopped

METHOD

1. Place the cucumber, coconut milk, water, lemon juice, zucchini, herbs and salt and pepper in a high-speed blender and process until smooth.

2. Serve garnished with chopped walnuts.

ZUCCHINI CARPACCIO

SERVES 4 ★ PREP 15MIN

INGREDIENTS

2 zucchinis

3 tbsps extra virgin olive oil

1 lemon, juiced

Sea salt and fresh pepper, to taste

½ cup (60g, 2oz) raw walnuts, chopped

125g (4oz) goat's cheese (see recipe page 8)

3 tbsps dill, chopped

METHOD

1. Slice zucchinis on the round using a mandolin or very sharp knife.

2. Drizzle zucchini slices with oil and lemon juice, and season to taste with salt and pepper.

3. Arrange on four dinner plates in overlapping concentric circles.

4. Sprinkle walnuts, goat's cheese and dill on top and serve immediately.

RAW PAD THAI WITH SESAME GINGER DRESSING

INGREDIENTS

2 zucchinis, julienned

1 carrot, peeled and julienned

3-4 small cauliflower florets

110g (4oz) white cabbage, shredded

1 red capsicum, seeded and sliced

1 yellow capsicum, seeded and sliced

1 green apple, thinly sliced

1 cup (30g, 1oz) lentil or mung bean sprouts

¼ red onion, sliced

Small piece of ginger, peeled and cut into matchsticks

1 lime, juiced

Sesame ginger dressing

¾ cup (120g, 4oz) raw, unhulled sesame seeds

½ cup (125ml, 4fl oz) fresh apple juice

⅓ cup (80ml, 3fl oz) orange juice

¼ cup (60g, 2oz) tamarind sauce

Small piece ginger, minced

1 lime, juiced

2 tbsps water

METHOD

1. Place the zucchini, carrot, cauliflower, cabbage, capsicum, apple, bean sprouts, red onion and ginger in a large serving bowl.

2. To make the dressing, place all the ingredients in a blender and process until emulsified. Add more water if required to reach desired consistency.

3. Pour dressing over the vegetables and toss to combine.

4. Garnish with Thai basil to serve.

SWEETS

AFTER DINNER MINT TRUFFLES

INGREDIENTS

½ cup (60g, 2oz)
raw cashews

¼ cup (90g, 3oz)
agave syrup

¼ cup (60ml, 2fl oz)
coconut oil, melted

½ cup (40g, 1½ oz)
finely shredded coconut

1 tsp peppermint oil

1⅔ cups (200g, 7oz)
raw cacao powder

METHOD

1. Place the cashew nuts in a bowl and cover with water. Set aside to soak for 3 hours. Drain and rinse.

2. Transfer cashew nuts to a food processor or high-speed blender and process until very smooth, scraping sides a few times. Add the agave syrup, coconut oil, coconut and peppermint oil and process again until combined.

3. Scrape the mixture into a bowl using a spatula and transfer to the refrigerator to chill for 1 hour.

4. Remove from refrigerator and roll into balls of desired size using dampened hands.

5. Place truffles on a tray lined with baking paper and return to the refrigerator for a further 15 minutes.

6. Sprinkle cacao powder onto a clean chopping board or work surface and roll the balls in the powder until nicely coated.

Note: Store in the fridge.

BRAZIL NUT BLISS BALLS

INGREDIENTS

4 cups (500g, 1lb 2oz) raw brazil nuts

½ cup (40g, 1½ oz) oats

½ cup (80g, 3oz) dried blueberries

4 tbsps sesame seeds

2 tbsps linseed

2 tbsps lemon juice

4 tbsps tahini

1 tbsp hemp protein powder

METHOD

1. Place the brazil nuts and oats in a food processor and process until coarsely chopped.

2. Add the blueberries, sesame seeds and linseed and process for a further 30 seconds.

3. Add the lemon juice, tahini, and hemp powder and process again until combined.

4. If needed, add a small amount of warm water until the mixture forms a firm paste.

5. Roll into balls using damp hands and then transfer to the refrigerator until ready to eat.

SNOW BARS

INGREDIENTS

2 cups (180g, 6oz) shredded coconut

½ cup (180g, 6oz) maple syrup

4 tbsps coconut oil, melted

1 tsp vanilla extract

¼ tsp sea salt

METHOD

1. Line a deep-sided baking tray or dish with baking paper.

2. Place all the ingredients in a food processor or high-speed blender and process until well combined and a slightly sticky consistency.

3. Scrape mixture into prepared tray and press down firmly to create a smooth and even finish.

4. Transfer to the refrigerator for 1 hour to set.

5. Remove and cut into squares.

   Note: Store in the fridge or freezer for up to one month.

RASPBERRY CHEESECAKE

INGREDIENTS

Crust

2 cups (250g, 8oz) raw almonds, pecan or walnuts

1 cup (175g, 6oz) soft Medjool dates

1 cup (90g, 3oz) desiccated coconut

1 tsp sea salt

Filling

3 cups (375g, 13oz) raw cashews, soaked

3 lemons, juiced

2 tsps vanilla extract

⅔ cup (160ml, 5fl oz) coconut oil, melted

⅔ cup (230g, 8oz) raw honey

2 cups (250g, 8oz) raspberries (fresh or thawed)

Coconut flakes for topping

METHOD

1. To make the crust, place the nuts, dates, coconut and salt in a food processor and process until the ingredients hold together and nuts and fruit have been chopped to the desired consistency.

2. Scrape the mixture in a mound in the centre of a springform plan. Press mixture down to form a flat base and then press up around the edges, ensuring that the mixture reaches into the corners and extends up the side of the pan. Place in the refrigerator while you complete the next step.

3. Place the filling ingredients except the raspberries and coconut flakes in the bowl of a clean food processor or high-speed blender and process on the highest speed for 3-5 minutes until very smooth.

4. Pour around two-thirds of the mixture into the prepared base.

5. Add raspberries to the processor or blender and process again until fully combined. Pour this over the filling. Top with coconut flakes.

6. Transfer to the freezer for 4-6 hours until solid.

7. Remove from the freezer 30 minutes before eating.

8. Use a very sharp knife warmed under the hot tap to cut.

   Note: Store in the freezer.

CRANERGY BALLS

INGREDIENTS

1 cup (90g, 3oz) oats

1 cup (160g, 6oz) dried cranberries

½ cup (65g, 2oz) raw almond butter (see recipe page 32)

1 tbsp linseed

¼ cup (90g, 3oz) raw honey

½ cup (60g, 2oz) raw almonds, crushed

½ cup (60g, 2oz) raw pistachios, crushed

METHOD

1. Place all the ingredients in a high-speed blender or food processor and process until well combined.

2. Add a little warm water, if necessary, to form a rollable consistency.

3. Using damp hands, roll into balls of the desired size and place on a tray lined with baking paper.

4. Place in the freezer until set, then transfer to an airtight container and store in the refrigerator or freezer for up to 1 month.

SWEET LINSEED BALLS

INGREDIENTS

10-12 pitted dates

1½ cups (185g, 6oz) raw walnuts

2 tbsps linseed

1 tsp vanilla extract

2 tbsps water

½ cup (80g, 3oz) sultanas

METHOD

1. Place all the ingredients in a high-speed blender or food processor and process until well combined.

2. Add a little warm water, if necessary, to form a rollable consistency.

3. Using damp hands, roll into balls of the desired size and place on a tray lined with baking paper.

4. Place in the freezer until set, then transfer to an airtight container and store in the refrigerator or freezer for up to 1 month.

PEANUT BUTTER BARS

INGREDIENTS

1 cup (125g, 4oz)
raw almonds

1 cup (125g, 4oz)
raw peanuts

½ cup (60g, 2oz)
sunflower seeds

½ cup (60g, 2oz)
raw hazelnuts

½ cup (80g, 3oz)
dried fruit

½ cup (65g, 2oz)
natural peanut butter

½ cup (125ml, 4fl oz)
coconut oil, melted

3 tbsps maple syrup

1 tsp vanilla extract

Topping

6 tbsps coconut oil,
melted

½ cup (60g, 2oz)
raw cacao powder

1 tbsp maple syrup

1 cup (155g, 5oz)
carob chips

METHOD

1. Place the almonds, peanuts, sunflower seeds, hazelnuts, dried fruit and peanut butter in a high-speed blender or food processor and pulse for 10-30 seconds, until the desired consistency is reached. Transfer to a large mixing bowl.

2. Place the coconut oil, maple syrup and vanilla extract in a small bowl and whisk until well combined.

3. Pour the wet mixture over the dry ingredients and mix with a wooden spoon until all ingredients are fully coated.

4. Prepare a baking tray or glass dish with baking paper.

5. Scrape the mixture into the prepared tray and transfer to the freezer for 30 minutes or until firm.

6. To make the chocolate mixture, combine the coconut oil, cacao and maple syrup in a small bowl and whisk until combined.

7. Immediately pour the chocolate topping over the bars and spread with a spatula. Top with the carob chips.

8. Return to the freezer for 20-30 minutes until the chocolate has hardened.

Note: Store in the freezer or refrigerator.

APRICOT COCONUT BALLS

INGREDIENTS

1 cup (190g, 7oz)
dried apricots

½ cup (85g, 3oz)
pitted dates

1 cup (125g, 4oz)
raw cashews

½ cup (40g, 1½ oz)
shredded coconut

½ tsp vanilla extract

Pinch salt

½ cup (40g, 1½oz)
coconut flakes

METHOD

1. Place all of the ingredients except the coconut flakes in a high-speed blender or food processor.

2. Process until the ingredients are fully combined and the mixture holds together when pressed. Process for longer to achieve a finer consistency.

3. Using damp hands, roll the mixture into balls of the desired size.

4. Sprinkle coconut flakes on a clean chopping board or work surface and quickly roll each ball in the coconut until nicely coated.

5. Transfer to the refrigerator to chill until ready to eat.

    Note: Will keep in the refrigerator for up to 4 weeks.

BLUEBERRY ICE CREAM

INGREDIENTS

2 frozen bananas

1 cup (100g, 3½ oz) frozen blueberries

2 tsps ginger, peeled and roughly chopped

¼ cup (30g, 1oz) cashews, soaked for 3-4hrs

2 tsps lemon juice

2 tbsps almond milk (see recipe page 10)

Fresh blueberries, to serve

METHOD

1. Place all the ingredients in a high-speed blender or food processor and process at high speed until creamy. Use the tamper tool to encourage the mixture to blend rather than adding extra liquid. If mixture is still too dry, add a little more almond milk.

2. Serve with fresh blueberries.

    Note: Store ice cream in the freezer and re-blend for 10 seconds before serving for extra creaminess.

CHOCOLATE MOUSSE

INGREDIENTS

2 ripe avocados, peeled and stoned

1 ripe banana

¼ cup (30g, 1oz) hazelnuts

4 tbsps cacao powder

2 tbsps maple syrup

1 tsp vanilla extract

¼ tsp cinnamon

½ cup (125ml, 4fl oz) water

METHOD

1. Place all the ingredients in a high-speed blender and process at high speed until creamy. Scrape down the sides as needed to blend all the ingredients together. If mixture is too dry, add a little more water.

2. Taste and adjust with maple syrup or cacao for greater sweetness or chocolatey flavour.

3. Serve immediately or transfer to the refrigerator to chill for 1-2 hours.

RED VELVET CHEESECAKE

INGREDIENTS

Crust

1 cup (125g, 4oz) raw macadamia nuts

½ cup (60g, 2oz) raw walnuts

½ cup (40g, 1 ½ oz) shredded coconut

Pinch sea salt

¼ cup (45g, 1 ½oz) pitted dates

Filling

3 cups (375g, 13oz) raw cashews, soaked for 2hrs

1 ½ cups (150g, 5oz) fresh cranberries

1 cup (250ml, 8fl oz) coconut oil

¾ cup (260g, 9oz) maple syrup

½ cup (125ml, 4fl oz) lemon juice

½ cup (125ml, 4fl oz) water

1 tbsp lemon zest

1 tsp vanilla extract

Pinch sea salt

Date and cranberry syrup

1 ½ cups (375ml, 13fl oz) warm water

8 Medjool dates

½ cup (50g, 2oz) cranberries

METHOD

1. Grease and line a springform cake tin.

2. Place all the ingredients for the crust except the dates in a high-speed blender or food processor and process until a crumb-like consistency forms. Add the dates and process again until well combined and slightly sticky.

3. Press the mixture firmly into the base of the cake tin. Transfer to the freezer while you complete the next step.

4. Place all of the filling ingredients into the blender or processor and blend until rich and creamy. Taste and adjust with lemon zest or sweetener, as required.

5. Remove the base from the freezer and pour in the filling. Cover the tin with foil and return to the freezer for 8 hours or until completely set.

6. To make the syrup, place the water, dates and cranberries into a blender and set aside for 30 minutes to soften the dates. When soft, process the ingredients thoroughly at high speed until a smooth, pourable consistency is reached. Thin with water if necessary.

7. An hour before serving, remove from the freezer and allow to thaw slightly.

8. Serve decorated with coconut flakes and cranberry date syrup.

Note: Store in the freezer and do not allow to sit at room temperature.

GO GOJI CANDIES

INGREDIENTS

1 cup (125g, 4oz)
raw almonds

1 cup (115g, 4oz)
goji berries

1½ cups (260g, 9oz)
pitted dates

¼ cup (30g, 1oz)
cacao nibs

½ cup (80g, 3oz)
hemp seeds

3 tbsps hemp seeds,
for rolling

1 tbsp goji berries,
for rolling

METHOD

1. Place the almonds and goji berries in a high-speed blender or food processor and process until a rough powder forms. Transfer to a large mixing bowl.

2. Place the dates and cacao nibs in the blender or processor until a sticky dough forms.

3. Place the date dough into the mixing bowl with the dry ingredients. Add hemp seeds and mix together by hand or with a wooden spoon. The mixture should be of a rollable consistency. If not, add a little warm water or raw honey to help it along.

4. Using damp hands, roll the mixture into balls of the desired size.

5. Sprinkle the hemp seeds and goji berries onto a chopping board or clean work surface. Roll balls through the mixture in order to coat well.

6. Transfer to the refrigerator to chill until ready to eat.

CHOCOLATE NUT TRUFFLES

INGREDIENTS

1 cup (125g, 4oz)
raw macadamia nuts

Water, as needed

½ cup (180g, 6oz)
maple syrup

1 cup (110g, 4oz)
raw cacao powder

Toppings

¼ cup (30g, 1oz)
cacao powder

½ cup (60g, 2oz)
chopped raw
macadamia nuts

METHOD

1. Place the macadamias in a food processor or high-speed blender and process until finely ground. Slowly add a little water and process again until a thick paste forms.

2. Add maple syrup and cacao powder and briefly process until combined.

3. Using damp hands roll the mixture into balls of the desired size.

4. Prepare a baking tray by lining with baking paper.

5. To prepare for rolling the truffles, clean and dry a work surface and sprinkle cacao powder and chopped nuts in two separate areas.

6. Roll the truffles in the desired coating and then place on the prepared tray.

7. Transfer to the refrigerator to chill for a minimum of 3 hours.

ROSE WATER CHEESECAKES

INGREDIENTS

Base

½ cup (60g, 2oz) raw almonds

½ cup (60g, 2oz) raw pistachio nuts

¾ cup (60g, 2oz) shredded coconut

⅓ cup (55g, 2oz) buckwheat groats

¾ cup (130g, 4oz) Medjool dates, pitted

3 tsps rice malt syrup

Pinch sea salt

Blueberry rose water cream

3 tbsps cacao butter, grated

1½ cups (185g, 6oz) cashews, soaked for 5hrs

⅓ cup (115g, 4oz) rice malt syrup

¾ cup (75g, 3oz) frozen blueberries

¼ cup (60ml, 2fl oz) coconut milk

1 tsp rose water

White chocolate cream

¼ cup (60g, 2oz) cacao butter, grated

1 cup (125g, 4oz) raw cashews, soaked for 5hrs

¼ tsp vanilla bean powder

¼ cup (90g, 3oz) rice malt syrup

¼ cup (60ml, 2fl oz) full-fat coconut milk

Grated chocolate and pistachio nuts, to decorate

METHOD

1. Place the almonds, pistachios, coconut and buckwheat groats into a high-speed blender or food processor. Process until fine crumbs form. Add the dates, rice malt syrup and salt and process until the mixture comes together in a dough-like consistency.

2. Scoop balls of the mixture into individual cheesecake or muffin trays and press down firmly. Transfer to the refrigerator to set.

3. Place the cacao butter for the blueberry rose water cream in a heatproof bowl over a pan of gently simmering water until melted.

4. Using a high-speed blender, blend the cashews, rice malt syrup, blueberries and coconut milk on low for 1 minute, then increase to a high speed for 2-3 minutes or until very smooth and creamy. Add the melted cacao butter and rose water and blend for a further minute until fully combined.

5. Pour the mixture on top of the cheesecake bases. Transfer to the freezer while you complete steps 6 and 7.

6. Place the cacao butter for the white chocolate layer in a heatproof bowl over a pan of gently simmering water until melted.

7. Using a high-speed blender, blend the cashews, vanilla, rice malt syrup and coconut milk for 2 minutes, or until very smooth. Add melted cacao butter and blend for a further 1 minute until very creamy.

8. Remove cheesecakes from the freezer and pour the white chocolate cream mixture on top.

9. Return to the freezer for 3 hours or until completely set.

10. Decorate with grated chocolate and chopped pistachios if desired.

CARAMEL TARTLETS

INGREDIENTS

½ cup (40g, 1½ oz) oats

1 cup (125g, 4oz)
raw walnuts

½ cup (80g, 3oz)
hemp seeds

2 tbsps chia seeds

2 tbsps shredded coconut

2 tbsps cacao powder

2 tbsps black sesame
seeds

2 tbsps maple syrup

2 tbsps vanilla extract

2 tbsps coconut oil

4 pitted dates

Frosting

2 cans full-fat coconut
milk (must have been
refrigerated for 2 full
days)

2 tbsps cacao powder

2 tsps maple syrup

1 tsp vanilla extract

To decorate

12 fresh blueberries

2 tsps cinnamon

METHOD

1. Grease a 12-hole tartlet tray with coconut oil.

2. Place the oats in a high-speed blender and process for 1 minute until a flour forms. Add the other ingredients for the base and blend on a high speed until a sticky dough forms.

3. Spoon the mixture into the tray and press down firmly with your fingers.

4. Open the coconut milk and discard the clear liquid on top. Transfer ½ cup (125ml, 4fl oz) of coconut cream to a large mixing bowl. Add the cacao powder, maple syrup and vanilla extract and stir well until a thick creamy mixture forms.

5. Use a spoon or piping bag to apply the frosting on top of the tartlets.

6. Decorate with cinnamon and fresh blueberries to serve.

SERVES 8 ★ PREP 25MIN (PLUS FREEZING)

RASPBERRY HEARTS

INGREDIENTS

¾ cup (90g, 3oz) almonds

7 Medjool dates

1½ cups (185g, 6oz) cashew nuts, soaked overnight or for at least 4hrs

2 bananas, frozen

4 tbsps maple syrup

½ cup (60g, 2oz) raspberries, roughly chopped

More raspberries to garnish

METHOD

1. Grease a 12-hole heart-shaped baking tray (or use a regular muffin tray).

2. Place the almonds and dates into a food processor and blend for a few minutes until a sticky dough forms.

3. Spoon the dough into the prepared tray and press down firmly until smooth and even. Transfer to the freezer to chill for 20 minutes while you prepare the filling.

4. Place the cashew nuts, banana and maple syrup in a high-speed blender and process until a smooth and silky. Add a little warm water if needed to thin the mixture.

5. Transfer the mixture to a large mixing bowl and add the raspberries. Stir gently to combine.

6. Remove bases from the freezer and spoon the filling on top.

7. Transfer to the freezer for 6 hours or until set. Decorate with fresh raspberries to serve.

CHOC-CHERRY CHEESECAKE

INGREDIENTS

Crust

2½ cups (310g, 10oz) macadamia nuts

½ cup (95g, 3oz) dried apricots

2 tbsps cacao powder

2 tbsps coconut oil

Filling

3 cups (375g, 13oz) raw cashews, soaked for 5hrs or overnight

½ cup (180g, 6oz) maple syrup

¾ cup (185ml, 6fl oz) coconut oil, melted

2 cups (400g, 14oz) strawberries, hulled

2 cups (400g, 14oz) fresh cherries, pips removed

¼ cup (60ml, 2fl oz) water

¼ cup (60ml, 2fl oz) lime juice

3 tbsps raw cacao powder

Cherry date syrup

1½ cups (375ml, 13fl oz) warm water

8 Medjool dates

½ cup (100g, 3½ oz) cherries

1 tsp lemon juice

Fresh cherries and finely grated lemon zest to decorate

METHOD

1. Prepare a round and high springform pan with baking paper.

2. Place the crust ingredients into a high-speed blender or food processor and process until combined and a sticky dough has formed.

3. Scrape mixture into the centre of the prepared tin and push evenly and firmly over the base to create a smooth and even finish. Transfer to the refrigerator to chill while you complete the next steps.

4. Drain and rinse the cashews. Place in a high-speed blender with the maple syrup and coconut oil and process for 1-2 minutes until well combined. Add the strawberries, cherries, water and lime juice and continue blending until creamy and smooth. Add the cacao powder and blitz for 10 seconds or so until mixed through.

5. To make the syrup, place the water, dates, cherries and lemon juice into a blender and set aside for 30 minutes to soften the dates. When soft, process the ingredients thoroughly at high speed until a smooth, pourable consistency is reached. Thin with water if necessary.

6. Remove the base from the fridge and pour the filling on top. Cover with aluminium foil and transfer to the fridge overnight to set.

7. Remove 20 minutes before serving. To serve, sprinkle lemon zest over the top of the cheesecake and then pour over the syrup. Decorate with fresh cherries

KEY LIME PIE

INGREDIENTS

Base

1 cup (125g, 4oz) raw cashews, soaked for at least 4hrs

1 cup (125g, 4oz) raw hazelnuts, soaked for at least 4hrs

5 Medjool dates

1 tsp coconut oil

⅛ tsp sea salt

Filling

3 ripe avocados, peeled and stoned

5 tbsps lime juice

1½ tsps vanilla extract

2½ tbsps maple syrup

1 tsp white chia seeds

To serve

1 cup (125g, 4oz) fresh raspberries

2 tbsps coconut flakes

METHOD

1. Place the ingredients for the base in a high-speed blender or food processor and process until a sticky dough forms.

2. Scrape the mixture into a fluted springform pie tin and press down firmly. Use your fingers to push the mixture up the sides of the tin as well. Loosely cover with aluminium foil and transfer to the refrigerator while you make the filling.

3. Place the avocados, lime juice, vanilla, maple syrup and chia seeds into a food processor or high-speed blender. and process until creamy and smooth.

4. Remove pie tin from the fridge and pour in the filling. Smooth the surface with a spatula to ensure an even top.

5. Decorate with fresh raspberries and coconut flakes and then transfer to the freezer to chill for a further hour before serving.

RAFFAELLO BONBON CUPS

INGREDIENTS

Base

¾ cup (90g, 3oz)
raw almonds

9 Medjool dates

Filling

5 tbsps coconut oil,
melted

1 cup (90g, 3oz)
coconut flakes

1½ cups (185g, 6oz)
cashew nuts, soaked
overnight or for at least
4hrs

3 tbsps raw honey

1 tsp vanilla extract

Garnish

12 whole raw almonds

¼ cup (20g, ¾ oz)
coconut flakes

METHOD

1. Grease a 12-hole mini-muffin tray with coconut oil.

2. Place the almonds and dates into a food processor and blend until
   a sticky dough forms.

3. Spoon the mixture into each muffin cup and press firmly into the
   base and sides. Transfer to the freezer while you complete the next
   step.

4. Place all the filling ingredients in a high-speed blender and process
   for 2-3 minutes until mixture is fully combined and creamy in
   texture.

5. Remove the cups from the freezer and pour in the filling. Transfer to
   the freezer for 3 hours or until completely set.

6. Remove from the freezer 30 minutes before eating and allow to
   thaw slightly.

7. Place a whole almond in the centre of each cup and sprinkle with
   coconut flakes to serve.

COCONUT BERRY CUPCAKES

INGREDIENTS

Base

¾ cup (90g, 3oz) almonds

4 pre-soaked dates

1 tsp ground cinnamon

2 tbsps maple syrup

3 tbsps coconut oil, melted

¾ cup (200ml, 7fl oz) coconut cream

⅓ cup (100ml, 3½ fl oz) coconut milk

Filling

1 cup (125g, 4oz) blackberries

½ cup (50g, 2oz) blueberries

1 tsp vanilla essence

1 tbsp desiccated coconut

1 tbsp maple syrup

2 tbsps coconut milk

1 tbsp coconut oil, melted

To serve

1 cup (125g, 4oz) fresh berries

2 tbsps coconut flakes

METHOD

1. Grease and line a 12-hole muffin tray with muffin liners.

2. Place the almonds and dates in a high-speed blender or food processor and pulse until a rough crumble forms.

3. Add the cinnamon, maple syrup and coconut oil and process again until fully combined.

4. Scrape the mixture into a large bowl. Add the coconut cream and milk and stir to combine.

5. Gently press the base mixture into the muffin liners and transfer to the refrigerator to chill while you prepare the filling.

6. Place all the ingredients for the filling in a high-speed blender and process until smooth and creamy.

7. Remove the bases from the freezer and pour the filling on top.

8. Return to the freezer for 1 hour until completely set.

9. Decorate with fresh berries and coconut flakes to serve.

CHOCOLATE BRITTLE

INGREDIENTS

200g (7oz) raw cacao butter

8 tbsps raw honey

¼ cup (30g, 1oz) raw cacao powder

⅓ cup (40g, 1½ oz) raw cashews, coarsely chopped

⅓ cup (40g, 1½ oz) raw pistachios, coarsely chopped

⅓ cup (40g, 1½ oz) raw walnuts, coarsely chopped

Pinch sea salt

METHOD

1. Line a shallow tray with baking paper.

2. Place the cacao butter in a heatproof bowl set over a pan of gently simmering water. Stir until melted. Set aside to cool for 5 minutes.

3. Add the honey, cacao powder and nuts and stir to fully combine.

4. Pour the chocolate into the prepared tray and transfer to the freezer for 1 hour until set.

    Note: Store in the fridge or freezer.

SERVES 2 ★ PREP 15MIN (PLUS SOAKING)

KIWI CREAM POTS

INGREDIENTS

4 tbsps white chia seeds, divided

1½ cups (375ml, 13fl oz) coconut milk

2 tsps raw honey

4 kiwi fruits, peeled and roughly chopped

To serve

1 kiwi fruit, peeled and chopped

METHOD

1. Place 2 tbsps of the chia seeds in a small bowl and cover with the coconut milk. Transfer to the refrigerator and leave to soak for a minimum of 20 minutes. Add honey and stir to combine.

2. Place the kiwi fruit in a high-speed blender or food processor and pulse to form a smooth puree.

3. Place the other 2 tablespoons of chia seeds in another bowl and pour the kiwi fruit puree over the top. Transfer to the refrigerator and leave to soak for a minimum of 20 minutes.

4. When ready to serve, evenly distribute the kiwi puree in the serving pots. Spoon the coconut cream on top and finish with fresh chopped kiwi fruit.

CARROT CAKE WITH CASHEW CREAM FROSTING

INGREDIENTS

Carrot cake

1 cup (125g, 4oz) raw walnuts

1 cup (175g, 6oz) pitted dates

½ cup (40g, 1½ oz) desiccated coconut

¾ tsp cinnamon

½ tsp nutmeg

Pinch salt

4 carrots, grated

Cashew cream frosting

1 cup (125g, 4oz) raw cashews, soaked for 4hrs or overnight

¼ cup (60ml, 2fl oz) water

3 tbsps maple syrup

1 tsp vanilla

Pinch salt

½ lemon, juiced

⅓ cup (185ml, 6fl oz) coconut oil, melted

Topping

Desiccated coconut

METHOD

1. Line a loaf tin with baking paper extending over the edges of the tin.

2. Place the walnuts and dates in the food processor and blend until nuts are fairly finely chopped. Add coconut, spices and salt and process to combine. Add carrots and process until fully combined, scraping down the sides as often as needed.

3. Scrape cake mixture into the prepared tin and smooth the surface with a spatula. Cover and transfer to the refrigerator to chill while you prepare the frosting.

4. Drain and rinse the cashew nuts and place in the bowl of a food processor or high-speed blender. Add the water, maple syrup, vanilla, salt and lemon juice and process for 5 minutes or until very smooth. Scrape down the sides as often as needed. Add the coconut oil and pulse to combine.

5. Remove the cake from the fridge and spoon on the frosting, then sprinkle over the desiccated coconut. Cover and transfer to the freezer for 2 hours until completely set.

6. Remove cake from the freezer and pull out of the tin using the baking paper. Set aside to thaw for 30 minutes before serving.

   Note: Midway through the thawing, cut the cake into the required number of pieces using a sharp knife run under a hot tap.

CHOCOLATE CHIA PUDDING

INGREDIENTS

1 cup (250ml, 8fl oz) almond milk (see recipe page 10)

3 tbsps chia seeds

1 tsp vanilla extract

1½ tbsps cacao powder

2 tsps maple syrup

Strawberries and sliced almonds, to serve

METHOD

1. Place the almond milk, chia seeds, vanilla extract and cacao into a jar with a sealable lid. Tighten the lid and shake until nicely mixed up.

2. Transfer to the refrigerator to soak overnight or for a minimum of eight hours.

3. When ready to serve, stir in the maple syrup and spoon into serving bowls. Top with fresh strawberries and sliced almonds.

PEANUT BUTTER BALLS

INGREDIENTS

12 pitted dates

1 tbsp raw cacao powder

2 tbsps natural peanut butter

¾ cup (90g, 3oz) raw almonds

1-2 tbsps agave syrup, honey or rice malt syrup, to taste

METHOD

1. Place the dates, cacao powder and peanut butter in a high-speed blender or food processor and process until a thick paste forms.

2. Add the almonds and pulse until desired consistency is achieved.

3. Add agave syrup in small quantities, pulsing between, to form a rollable consistency.

4. Using damp hands, roll into balls of the desired size and place on a tray lined with baking paper.

5. Place in the refrigerator until set, then transfer to an airtight container and store in the refrigerator up to 1 week.

TRIPLE-LAYER SUPERSLICE

INGREDIENTS

Red layer

2 tbsps chia seeds

1 cup (200g, 7oz) strawberries (fresh or frozen)

1 cup (115g, 4oz) goji berries

¼ cup (60ml, 2fl oz) coconut water

Brown layer

1 cup (125g, 4oz) raw pecans

1 cup (175g, 6oz) dates

5 tbsps raw cacao powder

4 tbsps shredded coconut

2 tbsps maple syrup

White layer

3 cups (270g, 9oz) shredded coconut

¼ cup (90g, 3oz) maple syrup

1 tsp vanilla extract

METHOD

1. Grease and line a deep-sided baking tray or dish with baking paper.

2. Place the ingredients for the red layer into a food processor or high-speed blender and process until a sticky dough forms. Add a little more coconut water if needed. Transfer to a small container and place in the fridge to chill while you prepare the other layers.

3. Place the pecans into a food processor or high-speed blender and process until a rough crumbly consistency. Add the dates and process until the mixture starts to hold together, then add the remaining ingredients. Process until mixture is well combined. Scrape the mixture into the prepared baking tray and transfer to the refrigerator to chill while you prepare the final layer.

4. Place the coconut for the white layer into a food processor or high-speed blender and process until the mixture starts to hold together. Add the maple syrup and vanilla extract and process until well combined with a moist and crumbly texture.

5. Remove the prepared layers from the fridge and assemble the slice. Spread the red layer on top of brown and finish with the white layer.

6. Transfer to the freezer to chill for 2 hours before serving.

STRAWBERRY ICE CREAM

INGREDIENTS

2 bananas, sliced and frozen

1 cup (200g, 7oz) strawberries, frozen

½ tsp vanilla extract

1 tbsp maple syrup

METHOD

1. Place all the ingredients in a food processor and blend until well combined and creamy.

2. Serve immediately or transfer to the freezer until ready to eat.

   Note: Will keep in the freezer for up to 1 month. Whizz in the blender to restore creamy texture after freezing if desired.

RAW CARAMEL SYRUP

INGREDIENTS

10 Medjool dates, pitted

1¾ cups (440ml, 15fl oz) warm water

1 tbsp fresh lemon juice

¼ cup (90g, 3oz) maple syrup

Pinch sea salt

METHOD

1. Place all ingredients in a high-speed blender. Allow to sit for 10 minutes until dates have softened slightly.

2. Blend on low until the dates start to break up and then increase to high speed until very smooth.

3. Pour syrup into a glass jar and transfer to the refrigerator until ready to use.

   Note: Can be stored in the refrigerator for up to 3 weeks.

CHEESEBOARD BALLS

INGREDIENTS

1½ cups (185g, 6oz) raw cashews, soaked for 4hrs, drained and rinsed

3 tbsps coconut oil

1 tbsp white wine

½ lemon, juiced

¼ tsp sea salt

Warm water, as needed

3 tbsps dried cranberries, chopped

¼ cup (30g, 1oz) raw walnuts, chopped

Toppings

½ cup (60g, 2oz) raw walnuts, roughly chopped

½ cup (50g, 2oz) dried cranberries, roughly chopped

1 cup (45g, 1½ oz) flat-leaf parsley, roughly chopped

METHOD

1. Place the cashews, coconut oil, wine, lemon juice and salt into a high-speed blender and process until smooth. If mixture is too thick to blend, gradually add warm water a teaspoon at a time.

2. Add the cranberries and the walnuts and pulse for 5-10 seconds until just combined. Scrape into a large bowl, cover, and transfer to the freezer to chill for 15 minutes to firm up slightly.

3. Line a baking tray or plate with baking paper. Set aside.

4. Prepare a clean and dry chopping board or work surface and sprinkle with the toppings.

5. Remove cheese from the freezer and, using damp hands, roll into balls of equal size.

6. Roll each ball through the toppings until completely covered.

7. Place balls on the prepared tray and transfer to the freezer to chill for 1 hour before serving.

RAWESOME COOKIES

INGREDIENTS

3 cups (375g, 13oz) raw almonds

½ cup (75g, 3oz) ground linseed

½ cup (60g, 2oz) raw cacao powder

¼ tsp sea salt

⅓ cup (80ml, 3fl oz) coconut oil, melted

⅓ cup (80ml, 3fl oz) water

½ cup (180g, 6oz) maple syrup

1 tbsp vanilla extract

1 cup (125g, 4oz) raw pecans, chopped

METHOD

1. Place the almonds in the food processor and process until a fine flour forms. Add the linseed, cacao powder and salt and pulse until just combined.

2. Add the oil, water, maple syrup and vanilla extract and process until thoroughly combined.

3. Transfer to a mixing bowl and stir in the pecan nuts.

4. Place a piece of baking paper on a clean work surface and use a rolling pin to roll out the dough to approximately 5mm (¼ in) thick. Use a cookie cutter to cut out circles of the dough.

5. Place the cookies on dehydrator sheets and into the dehydrator set at 45°C (115°F) degrees. Dehydrate for 48 hours.

   Note: You can also make these cookies in a conventional oven. Preheat the oven to 150°C (300°F, Gas Mark 2). Place the cookies in the oven and turn off the heat. Allow to cool completely.

BANANA NUT ICE CREAM

INGREDIENTS

4 ripe bananas, frozen

½ cup (65g, 2oz) raw almond butter (see recipe page 32)

¼ cup (90g, 3oz) maple syrup

½ tsp sea salt

¼ cup (60g, 2oz) tahini

1 tsp cinnamon

2 tsps vanilla extract

1 cup (125g, 4oz) raw cashews

Extra cashew nuts, to garnish

METHOD

1. Place all the ingredients in a food processor or high-speed blender and process until creamy and smooth, scraping down the sides as needed.

2. Taste and adjust with maple syrup if more sweetness is needed.

3. Garnish with additional cashew nuts and serve immediately.

   Note: To store, place in an airtight container and transfer to the freezer. Remove about 10 minutes before eating.

INDEX

HERRON
book distributors

First Published in 2016 by Herron Book Distributors Pty Ltd
14 Manton St
Morningside
QLD 4170
www.herronbooks.com

WWW.CAPTAINHONEY.COM.AU

Custom book production by Captain Honey Pty Ltd
12 Station St
Bangalow
NSW 2479
www.captainhoney.com.au

Cataloguing-in-Publication. A catalogue record for this book is available from the National Library of Australia

ISBN 978-0-947163-15-0

Images used under license from Shutterstock.com
Printed and bound in China by 1010 Printing International Limited

5 4   19 20

NOTES FOR THE READER

Preparation, cooking times and serving sizes vary according to the skill, agility and appetite of the cook and should be used as a guide only.

All reasonable efforts have been made to ensure the accuracy of the content in this book. Information in this book is not intended as a substitute for medical advice. The author and publisher cannot and do not accept any legal duty of care or responsibility in relation to the content in this book, and disclaim any liabilities relating to its use.